"If you quickly scan the chapter titles, you'll discover that you're doing the exact opposite of what Dara Duguay recommends in this book— which is exactly why you need to read it. If you adopt Duguay's commonsense ideas, you'll live a happier, richer life."

—*Ric Edelman, author of the #1* New York Times *bestseller* Ordinary People, Extraordinary Wealth

"I cannot think of an easier and better way to educate young people financially than to read and discuss with them a 'money rule' a day for two months. *Don't Spend Your Raise* is a uniquely valuable guide to financial well-being."

—*Stephen Probeck, Executive Director,*
Consumer Federation of America

"The autho... ..nversational narrative style, peppered with real-life anecdotes, makes this an easy yet informative read. You can pick and choose from the situations that sound familiar and learn from them. Reading and heeding the advice in this book is a great way to avoid making future money mistakes, without feeling judged."

—*M. Kathryn Kelly, Assistant Director, American Bankers*
Association Education Foundation

"As the NASDAQ Educational Foundation strives to promote education about financial markets, the free enterprise system, and smart investing, it helps to find young consumers who already have a good understanding and appreciation of basic personal finance. Dara Duguay's frank and sensible new book goes a long way toward laying this foundation of financial knowledge. Through examples and anecdotes to which young people will surely relate, she offers advice and warnings that will resonate with anyone who has ever saved, spent, borrowed, or invested."

—*Laura Levine, Director, NASDAQ Education Foundation*

DON'T SPEND YOUR RAISE

DON'T SPEND YOUR RAISE

AND 59 OTHER MONEY RULES YOU CAN'T AFFORD TO BREAK

DARA DUGUAY

Contemporary Books

*Chicago   New York   San Francisco   Lisbon   London   Madrid   Mexico City
Milan   New Delhi   San Juan   Seoul   Singapore   Sydney   Toronto*

The *McGraw·Hill* Companies

Library of Congress Cataloging-in-Publication Data

Duguay, Dara.
　　　Don't spend your raise : and 59 other money rules you can't afford to break /
　　Dara Duguay.
　　　　　　p.　　cm.
　　　Includes index.
　　　ISBN 0-07-140222-5
　　　1. Finance, Personal.　　I. Title.

　　HG179 .D8337　　2002
　　332.024—dc21　　　　　　　　　　　　　　　　　　　　2002073911

1 2 3 4 5 6 7 8 9 0　DOC/DOC　1 0 9 8 7 6 5 4 3 2

ISBN 0-07-140222-5

Interior illustrations copyright © EyeWire, Inc.

McGraw-Hill books are available at special quantity discounts to use as premiums and
sales promotions, or for use in corporate training programs. For more information, please
write to the Director of Special Sales, Professional Publishing, McGraw-Hill, Two Penn
Plaza, New York, NY 10121-2298. Or contact your local bookstore.

This book is printed on acid-free paper.

Contents

PART I

Investing in Your Future

PART II

Dollars and Sense

PART

III Livin' Large

PART

IV Credit: It's Not Your Money

PART **V**

Till Debt Do Us Part

PART **VI**

The Rainy Day: Finding Your Umbrella

Preface

As far back as my memory goes I was told, "Money doesn't buy happiness." I think my parents said this to make me feel better since our relatives were comparatively much wealthier. I didn't really believe them, though. One Christmas when my cousin got a car and I got a small, unmemorable gift, I definitely thought I would have been happier with my cousin's car.

My parents also sent me messages that the rich got that way by doing something unethical, which usually involved stealing from poor people—like us. Therefore, rich people would never be able to enjoy their money, since it was really ill-gotten gains. Somehow I doubted that the rich suffered the guilty conscience that my parents were certain was a consequence of their unscrupulousness.

Despite my parents' assurances that money would not buy me happiness or a guilt-free conscience, one thing that I knew for sure was that happiness could not be assured through poverty either. I decided that if I was going to be unhappy anyway, I'd rather be rich than poor. So I started my adult life in the pursuit of becoming rich. Since my first job out of graduate school did not pay me a salary that would make this pursuit a reality, I decided to supplement my income with cash advances from my credit cards.

This succeeded in giving me the illusion of wealth for a while, but eventually the unsustainable debt load exceeded my meager income. Thus began my long journey to getting myself out of debt. I am still amazed at how quickly you can get into debt but how long it takes to get out. This period of my life when I was constantly worried about my finances made me a believer in the adage "Money problems bring unhappiness." I found out for sure that even if material possessions could not guarantee happiness, debt certainly could guarantee the opposite—unhappiness.

This belief was maintained as I slowly got myself out of debt and became, for the first time in my life, not worried about how I was going to pay my bills. As my financial situation got better, I became happier! The joy that came from knowing that I was not constrained by debt and that I had savings to tide me over in case of a life event (an unexpected occurrence that results in an expense) was very liberating.

I would be a fool to promise you increased happiness as your wealth increases. But what I can promise you is that you'll increase your odds of being happy. If I was a gambler, this is a bet I would take any day.

Introduction

The average American spends more than he or she makes. At the end of 2001, the personal savings rate in this country plummeted to 1.6 percent, one of the lowest annual savings rates since the Great Depression. Accompanying the meager savings rate is an incredibly high debt level. American consumers now owe $7.3 trillion in total household debt. This is double the amount that was carried into the last recession. Heavy debt levels helped push the bankruptcy rate in 2001 to a record high of almost 1.5 million personal bankruptcies, surpassing 1999's record-breaking 1.4 million bankruptcies. Included among the 1.5 million were 94,717 petitioners age eighteen to twenty-five, according to the Consumer Bankruptcy Project.

This number may not seem alarming since it is only a small percentage of the total number of petitioners. But it normally takes years to accumulate an overwhelming debt level, and the fact that young adults are reaching this breaking point so soon is troublesome indeed.

The increase in bankruptcies has followed a trend. Over the past ten years, there has been a 40 percent increase in the rate at which American debtors filed for bankruptcy. These pessimistic statistics paint a stark reality: as today's young adults become financially independent, they risk replicating the mistakes of their parents' generation unless they learn to make smarter choices.

Regrettably, the financial literacy level of young adults has shown a decline over a five-year period. In fact, 68.1 percent of participating high-school seniors failed the Jump$tart Coalition for Personal Financial Literacy's third biennial financial-literacy survey. This was a huge increase from the 59.1 percent who failed in 2000 and the 44.2 percent who failed in 1997. The national survey of 4,024 twelfth graders found an average score of just 50.2 percent (an *F*) on the 31-question multiple-choice examination designed by a team of educators. This average score was down from 51.9 percent in 2000 and 57.3 percent in 1997.

It is expected that through part-time jobs, students will learn how to manage their money. In reality, only a small number (11 percent) of students save money for college or contribute toward family expenses (3 percent). Most adolescents use money for personal expenses (wants, not needs), such as clothing, cars, food, and entertainment. Manufacturers and advertisers are well aware of this fact and market heavily to teens and young adults.

If experience, or as I prefer to call it, "the school of hard knocks," is not the best teacher, then where should young adults learn about money? Their parents? Unfortunately, some parents feel uncomfortable discussing financial matters. Money is considered a taboo subject. Other times, the parents don't understand money matters themselves. Or the parents are skilled and competent financial teachers, but teenagers don't listen because they are naturally beginning to assert their independence and want to make their own decisions.

My parents used to give me lots of advice, but I ignored most of it. Ironically, I now occasionally hear their advice coming out of *my* mouth, directed at others. Many of us are recipients of advice that we ignore but then recycle after all. It seems that nobody takes advice—they just pass it on. Here's my first piece of advice: take my advice.

Since most people don't take good advice, by following mine, you won't have any competition. You could end up with vastly superior personal wealth just by following and not breaking my rules. Committing to my must-follow "rules" will enable you to manage your money better and increase your prosperity level.

Most personal finance books on the market are targeted toward the savvy money manager. Many of these books assume a basic level of financial competency in order to understand the contents. Many also focus on investing, and although more Americans than ever are investing in the stock market, the total percentage of Americans participating in the stock market is still only 48 percent.

The energy and time required to complete a detailed analysis of an individual's financial situation can be daunting and because of that, left undone. In contrast, *Don't Spend Your Raise: And 59 Other Money Rules You Can't Afford to Break* does not contain lengthy, complicated charts and equations to examine your finances under a magnifying glass. Instead, this book contains a system of dictates that, if followed, will guarantee fewer money mistakes and more money successes.

The "money rules" I present here are simple for even the novice money manager to understand . . . simple but powerful in their impact. *Don't Spend Your Raise* provides sound, proven, and easy-to-remember principles to follow in your financial life. You will become more confident in your financial decisions and ultimately more in charge of your financial future.

Don't Spend Your Raise is a friendly presentation of what must be done if prosperity is one of your goals. Since each money rule is separate but interrelated, you can conquer a rule a day or the entire book at one sitting.

You will learn rules like: Never Have More Than Two Credit Cards, Check Your Future Spouse's Credit Report, Never Buy a New Car, Pay Yourself First, Don't Wait to Win the Lottery, and many more.

We are all familiar with the saying "An apple a day keeps the doctor away." A money rule a day will (take your pick): keep the bill collectors away; help you save for a rainy day; and create wealth with which to play.

DON'T SPEND YOUR RAISE

Investing in Your Future

1

Don't Treat Money as a Taboo Subject

Open and honest communication is the first rule on the path to financial prosperity. If money is considered a taboo subject, not to be discussed, then the secrecy surrounding it may lead to unfortunate consequences. Not discussing financial goals or money troubles will likely ensure that your goals will not be reached and that your troubles will be exacerbated. Talking about money regularly will lessen the bickering and arguments about it and will encourage cooperation in attaining your financial goals and objectives.

While I was growing up, there were numerous taboos in my household. My conservative parents never talked about things that made them uncomfortable. This tended to mean any conversation that included sex, drugs, or money. But these are precisely the things that can cause us serious long-term damage if they are not understood and wise choices are not made.

Ignorance should not be a valid excuse for an unexpected pregnancy, a drug addiction, or a bankruptcy. Since information is the cure for ignorance, we should make it our duty to talk often and openly about money issues. This means talking regularly, not just when there is a financial crisis.

Try asking your friends and relatives if they've had any luck recently in the stock market. Chances are they will be proud of their investment successes and will want to share them with you. Retain and process this information, and then determine if their investment strategies are ones that you want to mimic. Hasn't it been said that stealing a great idea is the highest form of flattery?

If you are searching for life, auto, or health insurance, try asking your friends or colleagues if they are happy with their coverage. Do they feel they are getting the best rates for the service they're receiving? Did they comparison-shop before choosing their insurance companies? If you know someone who did an exhaustive search, he or she may be willing to share that research and save you countless hours of having to do the legwork yourself.

Similarly, if you are considering refinancing your home, talk to anyone you know who has just gone through the process. Did she have any criticisms about the mortgage lender or broker she worked with, or did she have nothing but praise? Did he feel he got the best deal available? In hindsight, was the decision to refinance a prudent one, considering the required closing costs?

As you can see, opportunities to discuss everyday money matters are always present. But the money taboo causes these occasions to pass by, unused. We prefer to ignore money discussions until we are confronted with a financial crisis. But more often than not, by the time a situation has become a crisis, it's too late for a desirable solution. There's no better illustration of this point than the story of John, a recent college graduate whose first full-time job was a low-paying, entry-level one.

John tended to procrastinate when it came to his finances. He typically paid bills only after receiving a second notice. He frequently had to pay late fees and even had his phone service and electricity turned off several times when he was extremely delinquent. John was not forgetful; he purposely stalled on paying his bills because he was waiting for another paycheck to hit his account. He was not living paycheck to paycheck; he was living on future paychecks!

John's friends would question him when they tried to call him and his phone was disconnected or when he slept on their couch because his place was without electricity. But John would always reply that his check must have gotten lost in the mail or the phone company must have made a mistake. His friends might have believed these excuses once or twice, but soon they saw that this was a common occurrence for John. When pressed about it, John became defensive and refused to talk about it.

To a professional credit counselor, John's situation was a simple one of living above his means. His expenses obviously exceeded his income. A solution might have been worked out by creating a budget for John to live within each month. This would have guaranteed that he wouldn't run out of money.

But since John wouldn't even admit that he had financial problems, he never sought a financial counselor. Eventually, his situation deteriorated to the point where he was evicted from his apartment and had to move back in with his parents. The next time he decides to move out, John will find it very difficult because his credit report will not be pretty. And there's no guarantee that the second time around will be any different from the first. Since John never actually admitted to himself or anyone else that he had financial problems, he won't be able to take advantage of learning from his mistakes. The only hope that John has of not repeating his previous mistakes is to break down his defenses and talk about his financial situation.

The message of money as a "taboo" subject is supported whenever we hear statements like "It's not polite to talk about money" or "I can't tell my friends I can't afford to go to that restaurant." Instead of agreeing whenever you hear these statements, try to resist their messages and replace them with "What's the big deal? Talking about money is perfectly acceptable and healthy."

While adjusting to the idea that money is not taboo, be patient. Ingrained ideas about money can be very strong, especially if they've been reinforced over the years by your parents. Start small and before you know it your discomfort with discussing financial matters will have disappeared.

2

Don't Fly First Class Just for the Free Drinks

Do you ever find that your spending habits just don't make sense? Think about it. For example, many of my business colleagues admit that they've upgraded airplane tickets just to get a few free drinks, yet the cost of upgrading far outweighs the cost of the drinks if they were to pay for them in coach. Here's another example: paying the cable premium each and every month so you'll receive hundreds of channels that you'll never watch because you're rarely at home to watch television. And what about that health club membership that you religiously pay for each month but haven't used in years?

My favorite example is my friend Nicole, who continues to pay a monthly membership for an expensive dating service even after the service apparently worked. The proof is Mark, with whom she's been in a committed relationship for eight months now. In fact, they're crazy about each other.

When Nicole told me that she hadn't stopped her membership, I asked her why. She replied that you never know what direction life can take, so she wanted to leave her options open. Nicole was not using the service anymore, but she still wanted to have it available if she decided to use it again. I told her that she could always rejoin after canceling if her relationship with Mark didn't work out. It's a waste of money to continue paying for a service that you're not using.

Even though my argument made excellent financial sense, Nicole simply would not change her mind. I then realized that spending decisions are either driven by logic or emotion. In Nicole's case, her emotional reasons were stronger than my logical ones.

If you find yourself making money decisions that are clearly not financially prudent, you need to first of all realize that fact. Then try to become aware of other monies that are not spent wisely. Look for all examples of expenditures that outweigh the benefits received. The challenge is to weigh the costs against the gains. Once you have identified these expenditures, resign yourself to stop paying for them. The ones that you resist giving up are going to be the ones that you are emotionally connected to.

When I examined in more depth my colleagues' reason for flying first class, some eventually admitted that they liked the flight attendants being attentive to their needs and the feeling of privilege that first class conveyed. In their case, the need for heightened self-worth merited the cost of the first-class seat. Unless this need to feel privileged disappeared, the need to fly first class would govern their spending decisions. Unless my friend Nicole develops a sense of assuredness that her relationship with Mark will be a long-lasting one, she will continue to rely on the dating service to provide her with an immediate backup.

Sometimes emotional reasons are stronger than logical ones. In spite of realizing why you do what you do, you still don't stop some irrational spending. This is all right . . . don't beat yourself up. Just be aware that if you need to cut down on your expenses one day, these are the expenses that should be targeted.

3

Don't Rely on Your Relatives for Financial Aid

Expecting your family or relatives to support you financially throughout your life is a way to ensure that you'll never be truly independent. You may be a grown-up in all other ways, but if you're dependent on them for money, you really are a "financial infant." True adulthood can never be achieved unless you overcome this dependency.

By being a financial infant and never taking full responsibility for your own finances, you'll always be running to your relatives for help whenever you need money. This is a pattern that Jessica had grown accustomed to . . . a pattern that she found increasingly difficult to break.

It started at an early age when she would run out of her allowance before next week's allowance was paid. She would beg her parents for the allowance early, and they'd have a hard time turning her down. Her begging became an art form that she was really good at, so good in fact that she sometimes received double the allowance she should have in one month's time. Jessica learned to rotate begging to her father and then to her mother so they didn't realize that the other had relented and had given her an advance.

As she got older, she started to acquire financial responsibilities. First it was her own cell phone (supposedly for emergencies only). Well, Jessica had a broad definition of what an emergency was, and before she knew it she had talked her way into a very expensive monthly bill. She cried to her parents and they paid the bill. When her next bill was equally excessive, her parents again paid it but took away the cell phone.

She then graduated to more sophisticated financial transactions. She got her first car. Her parents paid the down payment but required Jessica to make the monthly payments. She was working part-time while in high school, so she had more than enough income to cover the payments—at least this was her parents' theory.

The reality was that Jessica spent most of her income on frivolous things like clothes at the mall, eating out with her friends, and going to concerts. When it came time to pay the car payment, the money had disappeared. Her parents again came to the rescue since they didn't want her car repossessed. This would have resulted in a very negative mark on her credit report, which would have haunted her for seven long years.

This pattern of financial crisis and then parental rescue continued on as Jessica grew up. She had crises with her rent, her credit cards, and her parking tickets (which she neglected until the late fees made them exponentially more expensive than if she had paid them immediately). The need for money was constant and ever-increasing, but her parents continued to bail her out.

The end to this story is yet to be determined since the precedent has yet to be altered. I can make an educated guess, however. My feeling is that as long as her parents reward Jessica's irresponsible money management, it will continue. What incentive does Jessica have to change her behavior? It's much easier to call Mom and Dad whenever she needs money. That solution is infinitely much less painful than confronting the creditor.

But the money behaviors and decisions that continue to get you into trouble will not be forced to change if there is always a bailout waiting. It may become an endless cycle of dependency. You may spend your life having to rely on your parents for financial assistance, not to mention the burden that you are placing on them.

In addition, the assumption that family will always be there to take care of you financially can prove to be mistaken. The money tap may one day be turned off (if your parents somehow decide "enough is enough"), or the inheritance you fully expect to receive may not be your parents' intention. Therefore, self-reliance is the best way to assure you will be taken care of. For who cares more for you than yourself?

4

Write Down Your Money Goals

A goal that remains in your mind only is not an achievable goal. Just thinking about wanting to accomplish something is not enough. If we never write down a goal, it can never make the transition to being fulfilled. It's the difference between dreaming and goal-setting. And how many dreams actually come true? A goal can be accomplished while a dream is something to be longed for.

The best way to accomplish a money goal or objective is to write it down. The simple act of putting the goal on paper increases its success rate immensely. It may seem hard to believe that the best way to increase your odds of succeeding at a goal is something as simple as writing it down. But once the goal is written down, the mind starts working on ways to make the goal a reality.

Beth wanted to buy a house. She was only twenty-two years old, but she knew that unless she started saving now, her goal of becoming a homeowner would never come to be. Beth's goal of buying a one-bedroom condominium was not unrealistic, but the down payment that would be required seemed to be out of reach.

Her salary was typical of a young professional just starting her career. Even though her current expenses were relatively low, she still found it difficult to save each month. Most months, the idea of saving was just that . . . a nice idea. Her paycheck was very popular; it seemed that everyone wanted a piece of it. After rent, food, utilities, gas for her car, and other essentials, her paycheck was gone.

Beth despaired that her dream of owning a house would forever remain just a dream. It was only when her friend Brian suggested that she work out a plan that Beth started to have hope. He offered to share the plan that had enabled him to buy a home. Brian figured that it worked for him, so it might work just as well for her.

This plan involved creating a budget that included "actual" spending. Beth's assumption was that her essential expenses (rent, food, gas, et cetera) left no money for savings. It was only after she tracked her expenses for a month that she realized she did, in fact, have extra money after the necessities were paid. This money was never available for savings, however, because it was spent on "nonessential" stuff.

These "wants" in her budget (as opposed to "needs") included things like entertainment, meals out with friends, happy-hour drinks, manicures and pedicures, and weekend mini-vacations. If Beth cut back on some of these nonessentials, she would indeed have money to save for her house.

The next step in her plan was to decide which categories of expenses she would choose to reduce or eliminate. These decisions were painful. Having to tell friends she couldn't meet them for happy hour or having to pass up a shoe sale were sacrifices for Beth. She had to keep reminding herself that it was a trade-off. She was giving up things she wanted now in exchange for something she wanted in the future.

Her initial goal was to save $200 a month. By reducing her spending, Beth met that goal. After she got a new, higher-paying job, she resisted the temptation to increase her standard of living. She kept her expenses the same but increased her monthly savings to $400 a month.

The next step in her plan was to meet with a housing counselor to figure out her price range for a home based upon her salary. The counselor determined that her salary could comfortably afford a $100,000 home with a 20 percent down payment. This meant that Beth needed to save $20,000.

At first this amount seemed impossible to reach, but her counselor calculated that her regular $400 monthly savings plus interest would add up to $20,000 in approximately four years. At her current pace, Beth only had two years to go.

The most important part of Brian's plan was the part that cautioned to "never deviate from the plan." This was a critical component, since Beth was often tempted over the next two years to step off her path. Her friends constantly complained that Beth was no longer any fun since she turned down a lot of their offers to go out and spend money (at movies, bars, malls, et cetera). But in spite of the pressure, Beth stayed steadfast in her resolve. She even taped a picture of a condo on her refrigerator to give her inspiration.

Two years later, Beth was the proud owner of a lovely one-bedroom condo. At her housewarming party, all her friends were jealous. They too wanted to own their own places, but their visions were only dreams. Beth had made her dream a reality by setting a plan in motion. It all started by putting her dream down on paper and transforming it into a solid goal.

The steps that Beth took are essential to reaching any realistic financial goal. Once a general goal is chosen, you need to start writing down steps in the process of achieving that goal. By breaking up the goal into manageable pieces, it does not seem overwhelming. Beth's goal of saving $20,000 seemed impossible when viewed as the total sum, but broken up into monthly amounts of $400 it suddenly became possible. Most goals are attainable if the will to succeed is present and the goal is not an impossible one to achieve.

5

Don't Allow Events to Get You off Your Plan

If you've gone through the effort to create financial goals and have a plan in place, try to stick to it. Often, events cause us to abandon our plan. A good comparison is to someone who has been on a diet and then splurges one evening by eating a fattening meal. This person might be so discouraged about falling off the diet that he or she abandons it altogether. Instead of looking at the event as a temporary setback, the person views it as a complete failure.

The same philosophy applies for financial plans. There will be times when events happen that cause you to be diverted from your original plan. In Howard's case, he felt his financial pattern was destined to be "one step forward and two steps back." He wanted to save money, but unexpected expenses kept interfering with this plan.

He couldn't believe how unlucky he was. One month his car needed new brakes. The next month his car was back in the garage because his air-conditioning stopped working. Just when he thought his luck had changed, he got a speeding ticket. In fact, he was going so fast that the police considered it reckless driving, and Howard was hit with a large fine. As soon as his automobile insurer found out, his rates were raised. Several months later his dog ate some chocolates that Howard had left out. Since chocolate is extremely dangerous for dogs to consume, Howard had to rush to the vet (after hours) to get his dog's stomach pumped. The bill was shockingly high.

Because of this continual stream of "unexpected" events, Howard's plan to save money was put on perpetual *hold*. His friends who were successfully saving for cars and their first homes must be luckier than he was, Howard thought to console himself. However, this conclusion was turned upside down when Howard discovered his friends had similar events in their lives.

His friend Stan had to pay a tree-removal company after a windy storm knocked down several large limbs of his tree. His friend Maria was in a car accident caused by a driver who didn't have insurance. She was forced to pay the deductible to get her car repaired even though the accident wasn't her fault. And his friend Robert, after doing his income taxes, found out he owned the IRS several thousand dollars.

To Howard's great surprise, despite all these unexpected events his friends still continued to save regularly. Even if they had to skip a month or two, they religiously started saving again as soon as they were able. It turned out there was no difference between Howard's friends' luck and his own. The difference was in how they planned for and responded to these events.

Even though these particular events were unforeseen, his friends anticipated a certain amount of these unexpected occurrences. Their philosophy was that it is foolish to believe that "life events" will pass you by. They happen to everyone, normally when you least expect it or when you can least afford it.

Because of their certainty, his friends had included these events as an actual budget expense. For example, in Howard's budget they would have included "car repairs" as a normal expense. If Howard had factored into his budget a small amount each month to cover car repairs, he would have had the money when he needed it.

Howard's friends also built up short-term savings accounts that could be used to pay for those truly "unexpected" events, like tree-limb removal. However, most events that we think are "unexpected" are really not surprises at all. For example, if Robert had met with his accountant to figure out exactly how many allowances he should have been claiming when he filled out his W-4 forms with his employer, he wouldn't have ended up owing any money to the IRS. You could also argue that Howard wouldn't have been stuck with the vet bills if he had anticipated that his dog would try to eat the chocolates. He could have placed them out of his dog's reach.

In addition to the way that his friends planned for events, they also reacted differently. They viewed these events as temporary setbacks in their savings plans. Howard viewed his events as unending and permanent roadblocks to his savings goal.

Controlling how you plan for and react to events will make a huge difference in your ability to stick to a financial goal. Of course if you lose your job or unexpectedly find out you are pregnant, these events will affect your plan in significant ways. However, this doesn't mean that your plan should be discarded; it should be reworked to take the new realities into account.

6

Talk About Money as Much as Possible

Two subjects that remain taboo in most households, never to be discussed, are sex and money. Many consider it impolite to discuss these topics. Others feel extremely uncomfortable dealing with such private matters. For these and countless other reasons, most people would rather discuss anything other than their financial or sex lives.

When it comes to money, however, the more it is discussed, the better it is understood. But people are embarrassed to ask questions if they don't understand a financial transaction. They feel that they should already know the answer. Therefore, they prefer to remain confused rather than risk the humiliation of letting others discover that they are not financially savvy.

The irony of this way of thinking is the assumption that others understand money better than you do. Actually, few persons have been fortunate enough to receive formal training in personal finance. You may believe your knowledge is lacking, when in fact it may surpass that of others.

Just because someone is a professional doesn't mean that he or she is a master in knowing how to manage money. Many high-income individuals are horrible money managers. Their financial bottom lines may be much worse than that of someone from a lower-paying profession. It's not how much you make but rather what you spend in relation to what you make that counts.

Tiffany married at eighteen and started a family immediately after her marriage. She had two children back-to-back and their needs consumed her. Her husband, Bob, encouraged this focus on their children. He believed that Tiffany's responsibilities should revolve solely around their children and their home.

Bob relinquished control to Tiffany where homemaking was concerned, but he refused to let go of control over any other aspect of their life. He made most decisions without seeking Tiffany's input. In the financial arena, Bob felt that since he was the breadwinner, all money matters were his authority.

Tiffany, now twenty-five, had no idea what the family financial situation was and had never even balanced a checkbook. In fact, she didn't even know where the checkbook was. She wouldn't know how to manage money even if she had some to manage. Bob gave her money weekly, the same way he doled out allowances to the children.

Whenever Tiffany brought up the question of their finances, Bob's favorite response was, "Don't worry. I'll take care of you." Tiffany interpreted this response as, "You can't take care of yourself." Over time she heard this message repeated enough that she grew to believe she was incompetent when it came to financial matters. Tiffany decided to stop asking questions and just have faith that Bob was the wiser when it came to their finances.

Tiffany's spending tastes were modest, and the allowance she received weekly from Bob had always been enough to take care of the family's household needs. Therefore she was surprised one week when Bob gave her a smaller allowance than usual. When Tiffany brought up the fact that he had mistakenly shorted her allowance, Bob replied that the lesser amount was not a mistake.

Her follow-up question caused Bob to get so angry and defensive that Tiffany quickly dropped the subject. When the next week brought an even smaller allowance, Tiffany again pointed it out to Bob. This time his response was intense outrage. He accused Tiffany of having no faith in him as a provider.

Tiffany reassured Bob that she had all the confidence in the world in his abilities. She then resolved to never bring up money issues again . . . no matter what. Tiffany stuck to her promise, even when her allowance dwindled further and her requests for money to buy toys and clothes for the kids went unfunded.

Tiffany only learned the extent of their financial troubles from the collection calls that started to come daily. One day a repossessor even came to their door looking for Bob's car. The next day their landlord posted a notice on their door announcing their eviction.

Bob could no longer hide his financial problems by not talking about them. By now, they were out in the open. He broke down and admitted to Tiffany that he had lost his job four months ago and had been too ashamed to tell her. He left the house every morning at the same time that he used to leave for work and spent the whole day searching for another job.

This story does have a positive outcome, in that Bob ultimately had to ease up on his controlling ways. It would require two incomes to solve Bob and Tiffany's financial dilemma. Tiffany got a part-time job around the same time that Bob found another job. Together, the dual incomes slowly turned their financial situation around.

Tiffany also insisted that Bob share all financial matters with her from that point on. Bob's tendency to maintain total control over every situation—financial and otherwise—had caused their marriage to become more of a dictatorship than a partnership. For them to start functioning as a team, Bob needed to begin sharing financial management responsibilties with Tiffany. She had him teach her how to balance their checkbook. She asked that Bob give her the bill-paying duties. Then they did a budget together and worked out a plan to pay down their debts.

After a while, talking about money started to become routine. It was no longer discussed only when there was a crisis. They started to identify family goals like college tuition for the kids and buying a home. Once they agreed on certain goals, they developed a savings plan to realize them.

This radical departure from their old way of doing things was simply the result of communicating about a subject that was previously taboo. "The more that money is discussed, the more it is understood" is an important truism. Resolve to talk about money as much as possible. Talk to your friends, your colleagues, your parents, your kids, and especially your financial advisor.

The importance of having a financial advisor cannot be underscored enough. Many people want to be the "CEO" of their own personal investment company, but they don't have the time or expertise to manage their own money (or are too emotional about it). Would you represent yourself in court or in an IRS audit? Would you fix your own plumbing or give yourself medical advice? For specialized advice, we normally go to a specialist.

The best way to locate a financial advisor is to contact an investment firm that has name recognition and a long track record. I suggest making an appointment and visiting the office. When it comes to developing a plan for your investments, I believe a face-to-face meeting is more effective than a phone conversation.

Ask the financial advisor as many questions as you need to in order to fully understand the services the firm offers. No question is a stupid one. Most importantly, make sure the advisor listens to what *your* goals are instead of steering you in the direction of his or her own self-interest (for example, the latest stock the office is pushing or the fund that gives the advisor the highest commission). Shop around and choose the financial advisor who will work best for your needs.

Obviously there are certain personal financial issues you will want to keep secret: if you share your salary with a work colleague, your coworker might find to his surprise that he is not making as much as you are. Also, your young children might not know to be discreet about sharing your salary with their friends on the playground. (As children become young adults, however, they should know both your income and your expenses in order to have a realistic view of the world before they leave the nest.) You might also choose to be selective about whom you tell the extent of your debt level to or the fact that you once filed for bankruptcy.

But financial tools such as debt-reduction ideas, investment strategies, and cost-cutting ideas are ideal topics for money conversations. The frequency of these conversations and the level of your prosperity will almost certainly have a direct correlation. The more the better.

7

Learn from Your Parents

Your parents were probably your primary teachers when it came to learning how to manage your money. The Jump$tart Coalition for Personal Financial Literacy found in their 2002 survey of high school seniors' financial literacy level that 61.8 percent learned about money from their parents. Only 15.6 percent learned in school, and 17.8 percent learned from experience in managing their own funds, which is really the trial-and-error method.

Since our parents are our primary money teachers until schools start to integrate personal finance education more often, we need to learn from them. Their lead is certainly better than the trial-and-error method, which unfortunately results in more errors than successes.

You might have been lucky and had parents who were the best money managers in the world, or you might have had parents who repeatedly filed for bankruptcy. Your parents' skills are really dependent on the teaching that they received. In many cases, that teaching was minimal or nonexistent. This may result in the blind leading the blind.

Regardless of whether they were good examples or not, you can learn a great deal from your parents. This is because lessons can be learned from your parents' failures in addition to their successes. The secret is understanding which of their money choices were wise and which were not. This distinction is sometimes not very apparent.

Anita always thought her parents were expert money managers. She had no reason to believe otherwise. They owned a home, two relatively new cars, nice furnishings, and the family took overseas vacations each year. Whenever Anita needed anything she was given money. She even had a used car waiting in the driveway as a present for her sixteenth birthday.

Anita's vision of her parents being well-to-do was not shattered until her senior year in high school, when she started applying to colleges. Assuming that tuition costs were not a concern for her parents, Anita chose expensive, private Ivy League schools as her first choice.

When she was accepted at two of her top choices, she excitedly shared the good news with her parents. Instead of sharing her enthusiasm, however, her parents could not hide their worry and trepidation. Not understanding why they were not equally thrilled (it was Harvard and Yale, after all), Anita asked if something was wrong. Their answer caused Anita to totally redefine her perception of her parents' wealth. She ended up learning that the appearance of wealth or lack of it can be an illusion that completely contradicts the reality of the situation.

Anita learned that it wasn't the fact that she was accepted by such excellent universities that made her parents worry. In fact, her acceptance gave them enormous pride. The worry came from the fact that they weren't able to pay those schools' exorbitant tuitions.

Anita never thought for one moment that her parents were not in a position to pay her way through college. She just assumed that they had planned for it like many of her friends' parents, who had started college savings plans as soon as their children were born so that when the time for college came, money would not be an issue.

Unfortunately, Anita's parents never made regular savings deposits to a college account. They chose instead to spend the full amount of their combined incomes each month. They intended to start a savings account, but their obligations to their mortgage, car payments, credit-card bills, and other daily living expenses always prevented it from happening.

Over time this steady accumulation of debt became a vicious circle of acquiring more debt just to be able to pay the existing debt. In fact, Anita's parents' precarious debt situation made bankruptcy look like an inevitability. Paying college tuition on top of their existing debt was not an option.

Anita was despondent after learning the truth, but she was also determined not to let money issues prevent her from attending Harvard or Yale. She started researching alternative financing methods for her education. She filled out student loan applications, applied for scholarships, and made inquiries into work-study jobs on campus. In the end, by employing a combination of all of the above, Anita was able to afford her first year of school. In addition, she planned on working full-time each summer to supplement her college costs.

Anita was well aware that she was at risk of falling into her parents' debt trap with her student loans. Because of her sensitivity to this possibility, she did not ask for the maximum student loan amount available to her. She kept the loans on the lower side and supplemented them with her scholarship and work-study money. Also, Anita stuck to only one credit card with a low limit and paid it off in full each and every month.

As Anita's story illustrates, even if you have parents that have managed their money unwisely, you are not destined to repeat their mistakes. Hopefully you can learn from them. For example, if your parents filed for bankruptcy from excessive credit-card usage, you can learn to use credit responsibly and not get in over your head. On the other hand, if your parents made savings an integral part of their money habits, then you probably have firsthand examples of how compound interest makes money grow.

Don't be afraid to ask your parents to share with you their biggest money mistakes and what they learned from them. They might not be comfortable sharing this information with you, but be insistent. Tell them that you value their experiences and need their direction. Then ask them to share their greatest money successes. They will probably be less resistant to share this information. Take their wisdom and use it to your benefit.

8

Money Isn't Everything

The relentless pursuit of riches may seem to be the essence of the American dream. In the game of life, many believe that the true winners are those with the most toys when they die. We strive for bigger and bigger houses, more expensive cars, Italian shoes, Rolex watches, designer suits, and every electronic device imaginable. We hope to forget the time when all of our possessions could fit into one carload.

But when you obsess about the acquisition of money and let it control your every waking moment, you have lost your perspective about life. Your life then becomes imbalanced. When money dominates all thoughts and actions, other areas of your life are pushed aside. You neglect your family, your friends, and even your health. The stress over money can then lead to lost friendships, divorce, and an increase in blood pressure, difficulty sleeping, or even a heart attack.

For Peter, money was everything. It defined who he was and gave him an identity. Without his wealth, Peter felt he would cease to exist. Because his self-esteem was in direct proportion to how much money he had, Peter constantly needed more money to build up his feeling of self-worth.

Because Peter saw himself only in terms of how much money he was worth, he expected women to judge him in those terms also. When friends warned him that his girlfriend was a "gold digger," Peter was not deterred; in fact, he anticipated it. Holly was *supposed* to be attracted to him for his money, for Peter and his money were one and the same.

Peter was not born into wealth; he was born into poverty. He grew up watching his family struggle financially. There was never enough to cover the family's basic needs. Compounding their struggles was the fact that his family was treated with disrespect. They were discounted, pushed aside. No one ever took an interest in them or rushed to service their every request. He learned to believe that being poor was like being invisible.

Peter made a solemn promise to himself as a boy that when he grew up, no one would ever ignore him again. This promise guided his every thought and his every move. It caused him to study excessively in order to get into one of the best universities. His studiousness paid off when he received a full scholarship to Harvard. As a student there, he was drawn to courses in business and finance.

Upon graduation, Peter's attraction to money led him to an internship at a large investment firm on Wall Street. It was there he noticed that the more successful a money manager was, the more respect he or she commanded. Peter had the revelation that the best way to never be ignored again was to become hugely successful financially.

This was his mission, and his game plan was to work harder than anyone else to achieve success. The same philosophy that had worked so successfully in his studies at school paid off again in Peter's business career. He steadily rose to higher and higher positions of authority in the firm. With each move up the ladder his income increased accordingly. As his income went up, so did his stature and respect. Peter's assumption had proved correct after all.

The respect accorded him was shown in many ways. It touched all aspects of his life, from the company driver that now chauffeured him to and from work, to the doorman who greeted him at his apartment, to the elite "Members Only" social club that accepted him with open arms, to the corner office with the breathtaking view of Manhattan through its ceiling-to-floor windows.

As his fortunes increased, so did his luck with women. They were in awe that Peter was able to get reservations at the hottest New York restaurants. These spots had reputations of being impossible to get into unless you were someone "special." The women were in awe of the expensive presents Peter bought them on a regular basis. They were in awe of the front-row seats to sold-out Broadway productions. And most of all, they were in awe of Peter's gorgeous loft-style penthouse apartment with interior decorating that would make most women envious.

Of Peter's many girlfriends, Holly was the one most in awe of him. For this reason, he asked her to marry him . . . despite the "gold-digger" concerns of his friends. Their wedding was a posh affair, which continued into their married life. Holly's tastes were expensive and insatiable. She was endlessly redecorating their home and shopping for clothes. When she took a break from these activities, she turned to planning expensive overseas vacations to Bali and Monte Carlo.

As long as Peter did well at the firm, these demands were easily satisfied. Unfortunately, his earnings weren't sustainable during the stock market plunge of 2000–2001. Peter's personal portfolio included many risky Internet start-up companies, which had shown incredible earnings during the last years of the twentieth century but had plunged during the recession.

Peter had not followed his advice to his own clients, which was to diversify their investments. His need to realize high earnings because of his lavish lifestyle led to his decision to concentrate most of his investments in risky stocks. This decision was gambling on his and Holly's future. They stood to either win big earnings or suffer big losses. Just as most gamblers lose at Vegas, the odds finally caught up to him.

Peter's greatest fear during this period was that when his lifestyle was scaled back, Holly would leave—just like the Porsche he was going to have to give up. Since his worth was tied up in what he owned and not who he was, Peter believed it was a certainty that Holly wouldn't want him anymore.

When Holly didn't leave but instead supported Peter through this period, he was confused. Why was she staying? What do I have to offer her now that my wealth is not what it used to be? Her answer stunned Peter. Holly said that Peter was worth more than any of the possessions they had acquired. He heard her but didn't really believe her. It was only when the downscaling began that he started to believe her sincerity.

After their Porsche was taken away, their social club memberships were given up, they stopped going to the opera, and some of their paintings were sold, Holly miraculously still stayed by his side. It was only then that Peter felt self-worth for the first time in his life. Holly had shown that what really mattered to her was Peter himself and not the wealth that Peter represented.

What Peter had initially mistaken for awe of his money was actually awe of Peter himself. Holly was impressed by his intelligence and drive more than the money that resulted as a consequence. It was true that Holly had expensive tastes, but when she had to choose between possessions and her husband, she did not hesitate to choose the latter.

Believe it or not, there is more to life than money. Most people find that true happiness comes not from possessions but from relationships. You may worship your Porsche, but does it cure your loneliness? You may have the most beautiful view from your balcony but no one to share it with. Of course possessions can bring pleasure, but can "things" provide the bonds that make life worth living? That's a tall order for something inanimate. Be careful that the pursuit of things does not destroy that which is more valuable than money.

Dollars and Sense

Don't Cure Boredom by Going to the Mall

The next time you're out shopping for fun, ask yourself, "What mood am I in?" You may find that you tend to shop when you are depressed, bored, celebrating, or lonely. If any of these moods triggers a spending spree, you need to realize you have a tendency to shop whenever that mood overtakes you. By identifying moods that increase your spending proclivities, you can be aware that your resistance during this period is low.

Until I did this exercise myself, I hadn't realized that I tended to shop when I was depressed. It actually made sense in the short run. Since my spirits brightened when I bought something new, I would mask my feelings of depression temporarily when I treated myself to something I wanted. However, my depression level usually dictated my level of spending. One time when I was severely depressed I bought a new car!

Of course, this feeling of happiness didn't last for long. As the newness of the purchase wore off and the credit card bill arrived in the mail, my depression returned big-time. It became a vicious cycle. I would get depressed, go shopping, receive the bill, get depressed because of the bill, and then go shopping again. It was a cycle that was hard to break.

Instead, I learned to substitute another activity instead of shopping to try and alter my mood. I knew from many years of being an athlete that the activity of exercising was also successful in making me less depressed. The body's natural reaction while exercising is to release chemicals that give you a natural high. A bonus was the fact that since I taught aerobics,

I was actually making money instead of spending it; and getting into shape, not into debt!

If the activity you substitute for shopping works just as well, you've accomplished the same mood change without adding to your debt. If you shop to celebrate, try celebrating by seeing a new movie (you're only out the cost of the ticket). If you shop to cure boredom, try indulging in a hobby. But make sure you choose a relatively low-cost hobby, not a high-cost one like skiing, for example. And if you are lonely, try joining a club so you can meet others. Your club activities may alleviate your boredom and depression at the same time.

Be careful that the substitute activity is not harmful to you in another way. You have only succeeded in trading problems if you choose to drink heavily as your method of combating depression. And if you sense that your moods are extreme (for example, chronic, debilitating depression instead of occasional feelings of being depressed), you should visit a professional to get counseling. No amount of substitution can cure a serious psychological problem.

13

Don't Carry Around Loads of Cash

If you leave the house in the morning with $20 in your pocket, chances are that it will be gone by the end of the day. If you leave your house with $50 in your pocket, it too will probably have disappeared by day's end. The moral of the story is "The more you have, the more you will spend."

When I was in graduate school in Paris, I received a work-study scholarship. In exchange for partial reimbursement of my tuition, I had to work for several hours each day in the school's office. The school that I attended was a U.S. university with numerous campuses in Europe. Unluckily for me, my scholarship check was sent to the wrong campus—in Germany.

By the time this mix-up was straightened out, it was almost four months into the semester. This was a huge problem since I had counted on my scholarship money to pay my living expenses in France. My rent was covered, but other expenses like money for the metro, food, toiletries, school supplies, and coffee were not.

I had no choice but to get by on less. I remember vividly that I lived on $50 for the last month before the check finally arrived. I also remember exactly what I ate each day—a croissant and a cappuccino in the morning, a ham and cheese sandwich and a cappuccino for lunch, and soup for dinner. I had never voluntarily chosen to go on a diet before, and all of a sudden I found myself forced to go on a stringent one. I did in fact lose ten pounds (the only good news at the time).

I also walked more and took the subway less. I borrowed other people's newspapers after they had finished reading them instead of buying my own. I even made an occasional "complimentary" phone call to the United States from the office when the staff was on their customary two-hour French lunch break.

Years later while living in Los Angeles, I watched with amusement as my struggling actor friends used similar tricks, like eating dinner each night at a different happy-hour buffet. They bought a beer and had dinner for free. However, they learned it was important to rotate restaurants in case the managers caught on to the frequency of their visits.

My experience in Paris and the experiences of my friends in Los Angeles were not easy by any means. But I did learn that we could survive within our limitations. I also discovered that as soon as my scholarship money arrived, I had no problem spending more.

With more money available, I didn't have to have the same self-discipline as before. I could order several-course meals at restaurants, buy clothes, take taxis, and go to museums on days other than the free day. Since I now had more money in my possession, I felt released from the necessity of comparing and always choosing the cheapest or free way.

The lesson I learned in Paris that semester was a valuable one. If I wanted to spend less, I needed to have access to less. The lesson works on the premise that "if you don't have it, you can't spend it." And in Paris, I really didn't have it. I had no choice but to live on my limited funds since I didn't have a credit card. So what I had in my pocket was really all that I had.

To make it difficult to spend money, don't carry it around with you. In addition to actual cash, don't carry around other means of access to money like your checkbook, debit cards, or credit cards. Leave them at home or have a trusted family member hide them for you. Then have them promise not to let you know where they are hidden, even if you beg. If you make it difficult to spend, you *will* spend less.

14

Never Buy a New Car

The minute you drive a new car off the dealer's lot, it has immediately become used and yours. If you have buyer's remorse (that sinking feeling that you shouldn't have made the purchase) a block away, you can't return it. Buying a car is not like buying a sweater at a department store and discovering it's the wrong size once you're home. In the case of the sweater, you can most likely return it and replace it with one that's a better fit. With a car, on the other hand, if you discover your eyes were bigger than your pocketbook, you can rarely return it for one that is a better fit with your budget.

The reality is that you have lost several thousand dollars in value before you even make it to your driveway. The simple act of driving your new car off the dealer's premises has decreased its value. Contrary to purchasing a home, the odds of your car increasing in worth are almost nil. This immediate depreciation was what caused Ron to find himself in an "upside-down" situation.

Ron was only twenty-five, but his drive to succeed put him in a self-imposed competition with salesmen at his company who were much older. Ron grew up lower middle-class in the suburbs of Cleveland, and he aspired for much more than what his parents had attained. This desire fueled his ambition.

Ron gravitated toward the most successful employees. He wanted to pattern himself after them, reasoning that if he did what they did, he would be as successful as they were. Therefore, he studied them—their work habits, mannerisms, clothing, and the type of cars they drove. It was in copycatting the cars his colleagues drove that Ron got himself into trouble.

It was unrealistic to try to compete with the older salesmen at every level. Ron didn't realize that it took time to accumulate wealth. It was true that many of his older colleagues drove luxury cars, but it was also true that they paid substantial down payments when they bought them. This enabled their monthly payments to be much lower than Ron's, since he bought his car entirely on credit. In fact, Ron's car payment was equal to his rent!

It didn't take long for Ron to realize that he couldn't afford his car. He wasn't that good at math, but it was easy to calculate that his monthly salary was just slightly more than his rent and car payment combined. This left a pittance to pay for everything else like food, clothes, cell phone, gas for his car, and other expenses.

Ron determined that the solution was to return his car. But when he tried to give it back, the car dealer wouldn't take it. They told him to try and sell it on his own. Ron followed their advice but discovered that the price he could sell it for was not enough to cover what he owed the lender. His situation was what is known as "upside down." If he sold it, he would be stuck paying the difference between the money he received and the money he still owed—this is called a deficiency balance. Even wo. he wouldn't have any transportation. He would then need to get another to get to work. This would effectively result in Ron paying for two vehicles but only having possession of one.

Feeling trapped, Ron decided to move back in with his parents until he could get his finances in better shape. This decision was not an easy one, since Ron had loved his independence. Now he was back in his parents' home, living under their rules when he was used to none. He lamented the fact that his situation wouldn't have come to this if he had only bought a used car.

When you buy a used car, the vehicle's greatest depreciation has already been realized by its original owner. All subsequent owners won't experience the huge plunge in value that the original purchaser of the new car had to realize. The goal should be to retain as much of the car's purchase value as possible. Buying a new car instead of a used one makes this goal less attainable.

15

When You Change Jobs, Don't Cash out Your Retirement Account

If you are like the average American, who doesn't save any money other than what he or she contributes to a retirement account, when you lose a job or change jobs you may find that you have no short-term savings to pay bills until you find that next job. In a competitive job market, it may take several months (if not longer) to find your next place of employment. While the search is going on, although your paychecks have ceased to arrive, unfortunately your bills have not.

In desperate need of cash, many people turn to cash advances on their credit cards. If their credit cards are already tapped out, they may attempt to cut back on their expenses. This scaling back is difficult because it involves giving things up, and many people resist that temporary solution. A less painful option is looking to their company retirement account as an interim source of funds. An employee who has worked for a company for a long time, or whose company is particularly generous in matching employee contributions, may find that his or her retirement account is quite substantial.

In fact, the majority of Americans cash out their 401(k) balances when they change jobs rather than rolling over the money into another retirement account, according to a recent study conducted by Hewitt Associates, a management consulting firm. The Hewitt study revealed that more than 80 percent of employees cash out when balances are $3,500 or less. Even among those with larger balances of $25,000 or more, 30 percent choose to cash out their funds.

This was Sam's preferred solution to his temporary cash crunch after he was laid off from his job with a telecommunications company. He knew that he had no accessible short-term savings since he habitually lived from paycheck to paycheck. Further, Sam was unwilling to cut back on some of his expenses because it was a hassle to do a budget and then have to decide which expenses to reduce or eliminate. After these difficult and time-consuming decisions, he would then have to make lots of phone calls to cancel services. This seemed like way too much work and effort. Besides, Sam felt that adjusting his budget was entirely unnecessary for his short-term problem.

Sam had accumulated around $4ʊ,ʊʊ0 in his company 401(k) plan by the time of his layoff. During an exit interview with the company personnel director, he received advice about his 401(k) plan. The personnel director explained something about it being advisable to roll over his funds into another retirement account within a short period.

Sam really didn't understand what she was explaining about a "rollover," so he elected to receive a check equal to the amount in his account instead. This freed up $45,000, and suddenly Sam didn't feel such an urgency to find his next job right away. In fact, he had always wanted to visit Europe.

Sam's European excursion lasted three months before he returned home to start his job search. It took an extra three months before he found employment and began receiving a paycheck again. He had been out of work for a total of six months but hadn't really felt any money pressure during this time, thanks to his retirement funds. In fact, Sam felt that his layoff was a wonderful gift.

It wasn't until he met with his accountant to do his taxes that Sam realized the significance of what his former personnel director had been advising him to do. Since he did not elect to "roll over" his retirement account into another, similar fund, he was severely penalized by the IRS. Unfortunately, Sam realized too late the negative consequences of electing to cash out his retirement fund. He ended up losing about $20,000 by the time the taxes and penalties were calculated. His European vacation turned out to be quite an expensive one!

The decision to cash out your retirement account instead of rolling it over to your new company's retirement plan or your individual retirement account (IRA) will result in a significant reduction in the net value of the account. By the time you have been taxed and penalized for an early withdrawal, which usually is defined as any disbursement before age fifty-nine and a half, approximately half of the value of your withdrawal will have vanished. And in the long term you lose even more because you forfeit the tax-deferred compounding of the retirement account's earnings.

Oftentimes, people in their twenties look at the lump sum in their plan and decide that retirement is a long way off, so they would rather have the money to pay bills or use for a down payment on a car. If your argument is that your need for the money is greater now rather than later in life, you should first see if the fund has a borrowing provision. It may allow you to borrow from the fund for certain reasons like an emergency or a down payment on a home. Other funds have no restrictions at all on borrowing.

If this course of action is allowable, you have in essence taken out a loan against your retirement funds. The difference from an outright cash distribution is that you have a repayment plan to replace the money that you have received. In addition, you will not be hit with huge penalties for early withdrawal like you would if you received a check from liquidating your account.

The loss of money through penalties and taxation is easily avoidable by making sure to always roll over your company retirement account whenever you switch jobs. Since frequent job-changing is becoming the norm, it is imperative to make this choice. If you don't, you'll never be able to accumulate any money for retirement. You may find yourself forced to live solely on social security income. Let's hope that social security is not out of money by the time you need it.

16

Don't Take a Vacation in High Season

To guarantee the highest rates for airfare, hotel accommodations, and vacation excursions, you only need to book your travel during peak tourist season. In addition to paying premium rates for everything you do, you will be assured of lots of company. Most people prefer to travel in high season since it is usually the most desirable time to travel.

Peak season is determined by many factors. If it is during the winter, warm destinations are in demand. You can count on Mexico and the Caribbean being very crowded. If it is during summer break for kids, families will be plentiful at many destinations—especially family-friendly places like Disneyland. If you are planning on visiting the Mediterranean coast in Europe, it will seem like virtually all of Europe has joined you.

Helen had heard tales of how wonderful St. Barthélemy (St. Barts for short) was for years. The picturesque island in the French West Indies is a favorite destination of many famous people. It seemed that every time Helen picked up a *People* magazine, she saw pictures of movie stars on holiday in St. Barts. She wanted to join them in what was obviously an extremely desirable vacation spot.

Helen's enthusiasm for visiting St. Barts was matched only by her excitement at escaping Michigan in January. As she waited on hold to make her plane reservations, she looked outside at the three feet of snow, which was supposed to accumulate to four feet by nightfall. In addition, the high temperature predicted for the day was only five degrees. Helen reflected at that moment that her trip couldn't come soon enough.

Helen had a hard time convincing friends to join her because the cost of the trip was quite expensive. She was booking her trip during high season, and the airfare, hotel, rental car, and excursion packages were at their highest rates. No discounts applied for this time of the year.

The trip turned out to be everything that Helen was hoping for. When she arrived home, her stories of "movie-star sightings" and beautiful white-sand beaches caused her friends (who had initially turned down r offer to come along) to rethink their decision. So Sara and Jennifer started doing some preliminary research to see if they could afford the trip.

They discovered that April 15 was the cutoff between high and low season. If they booked their trip after April 15, they would receive huge discounts on airfare, hotels, and many other trip-related expenses. Their airfare was dramatically lower than high-season rates, and they were even able to negotiate a half-price reduction for their hotel room since the hotel had such low occupancy. Once there, they were able to bargain for reduced rates for scuba diving, sailboat, and hiking trips. An added benefit was that they were often the only tourists on these excursions, so they received extra attention.

When Sara and Jennifer returned to Michigan they kept marveling at the affordability of St. Barts. Helen was confused because her trip had been so expensive that she was force .t most of the expenses on her credit cards just to be able to affo .o go. She calculated that she would be paying off her credit cards for the next year or so just to pay off that one week. How could her friends' experience have been so different?

The difference was in the fact that one trip occurred during high season and the other during low season. Although Sara and Jennifer didn't see one movie star while they were there and the temperature was much hotter than during Helen's trip, they thought the trade-off was acceptable in order to receive such low fares.

In fact, they looked at the fact that the island had so few tourists as a definite plus. By traveling off-season they were guaranteed fewer crowds and more solitude. They never had to wait in line for a table at a restaurant, and one day they were the only ones on the beach for two hours.

If you are willing to accept less-than-optimum conditions, you may save big bucks. If you are willing to be flexible you can find some great deals: hurricane season in the Caribbean is cheap, winter in London is an inexpensive plane flight away, and August will find Paris seemingly deserted since the Parisians are on the Riviera.

I have a friend who only travels to places that are dangerous. In fact, that is how he chooses his destination. He will travel to a country in the midst of an uprising, a political or social upheaval, or with a high kidnapping rate for foreigners. He swears that he receives the lowest rates for any vacation. I don't doubt that he does receive low rates, but he is too much of a gambler for me. I prefer to choose vacation destinations with a high degree of certainty that I will return home!

A vacation should reduce your stress level, not add to it by increasing your fear of kidnapping or by adding to your financial stress. If an expensive vacation prevents you from enjoying yourself, then the vacation has not accomplished its intended goal.

17

Never Make a Significant Purchase on the First Trip to the Store

When you need to make a significant purchase, the decision should not be made in haste. Never commit yourself to a purchase on the first trip to the store, even if your emotions cause you to consider otherwise. The irrational or emotional mind often prevails over the rational mind when it comes to spending money. If the power of your emotional mind goes unchecked, your logical mind will be the underdog in the battle over purchasing decisions. This can cause you to make purchases you come to regret.

A common example of an emotionally based purchase is a vacation time-share. Steve and Aileen would be the first to admit that their decision to buy a time-share in Mexico was purely an emotional one. They were in Cabo San Lucas for a long weekend, making the short flight from Los Angeles. The trip was laced with sentiment since Steve proposed to Aileen while they were there. She quickly accepted and they knew that Cabo would always have a special place in their hearts.

They were therefore good candidates (from a salesman's perspective) when they decided to attend a time-share presentation. They only agreed to attend because they were promised a free rental car for the day. Once there, however, they were caught up in the moment and didn't put up any resistance when the hard-sell part of the presentation arrived. They signed on the dotted line and promptly became owners of a time-share in Cabo.

It was only when the reality of what they had committed to became apparent that they had second thoughts. Both Steve and Aileen were adventurous and loved traveling to different places. But with the time-share they had purchased, they were stuck with vacationing all the time in Cabo. They could have chosen other destinations, but the guilt they would have felt over paying for a time-share they didn't use—in addition to having to pay the vacation expenses related to another destination— would have been too great.

Compounding their aggravation was the fact that the time-share property was not theirs alone. It had been sold to many others, and their time was limited each year depending on its availability. Aileen and Steve tried to book the time-share several times when they both were available, but the time-share unfortunately was not. They mournfully acknowledged that it would have been easier to book a room at any of the numerous beautiful resort hotels in Cabo.

Over time their fond memories of Cabo became replaced with the sense that they were trapped in a situation they couldn't get out of. Finally they decided to sell their time-share. In the end, their calculations over what they spent on the time-share revealed a depressing truth. They would have saved money if they had made hotel reservations on a per-trip basis. And they would have been able to visit different countries as well.

Consider your initial sales visits to be for research purposes only (comparing and contrasting prices and features). The first trip is heavily laden with emotion instead of rationality. When you first view that car you must have or that home that is perfect for you, you are not thinking clearly. All you are thinking about is how much you would love to drive that car or live in that home. Your mind is crowded with visions of road trips or dinner parties with your friends.

Added to these visions is a sense of urgency that many salesmen employ in order to close the deal. They make you believe that these dreams can only become reality if you "act now." For if you hesitate and go home to think it over, in your absence someone else will make an offer on your dream house and you will have lost your opportunity.

Therefore, in your rush to acquire the item before it is gone and someone else has swooped it away from you, you might skip over the careful consideration that a significant purchase warrants. It is imperative to get the facts and figures and go home and then make an analytical decision, removed from the temptation. If after you've done all the calculations you find you still want the item, then return and buy it.

It is rare that you will have lost a golden opportunity. More times than not, there will be a multitude of other time-shares to choose from, other houses to buy that you would be equally content with, or other car dealers that have the exact car you have decided on. In our consumer society, a shortage of goods is usually not a common problem.

18

Pay Your Mortgage Biweekly

By altering your mortgage payment schedule (assuming you pay monthly), you can cut the total amount you pay on your loan significantly over its lifetime. In addition to the savings you will have gained is the added benefit of shortening the length of your loan. You need to simply pay half your monthly mortgage payment biweekly.

This offer came in the mail to Alec from his mortgage lender. He liked the idea of saving money and time, but even more he liked the idea of not having to write any more checks to his mortgage lender. The biweekly offer included an automatic withdrawal every two weeks from his checking account of half the amount of his mortgage payment. No longer did Alec have to worry about having his mortgage check arrive on time. This was initially his main motivation to start the biweekly plan.

Alec lived a hectic, busy life, and bookkeeping was not one of his strengths. It seemed he regularly missed the due date on his mortgage payment and had to pay a late-fee penalty the next month. On his mortgage of $1,500, the late fee was $150! He estimated that he probably paid an extra $1,000 a year in late-fee penalties. This was basically wasted money since he derived no benefit from it and couldn't even claim it as an additional mortgage deduction when he did his income taxes.

Alec didn't initially understand how he could save time and money (he didn't read the mortgage lender's brochure, except for the automatic payment section), but after one year on the plan he understood. Since there are twenty-six biweekly periods in a year, each year you will have made the equivalent of one extra mortgage payment. In contrast, if you continued to pay monthly but cut your payments in half, you would only make twenty-four payments a year.

That extra payment goes to reduce your principal instead of just covering the interest. For that reason you can powerfully attack the total cost of your mortgage. For instance, on a $100,000 mortgage at a 10 percent interest rate, you can save $83,000 in scheduled payments and knock ten years off the life of your thirty-year mortgage. Without a biweekly payment plan, however, you would still owe $63,740 at the end of twenty years instead of owning your home free and clear.

An additional advantage is that the $83,000 in savings could instead be invested and work for you instead of against you. If your investment earned an interest rate of 10 percent, your yield would be $160,000 after thirty years. These investment earnings far outweigh any savings you could realize from the tax benefit on your interest deduction.

Alec was excited about the prospect of paying off his mortgage early. The thought of having to work into his sixties before he retired was just too depressing to contemplate. He had plans to retire early, and this plan was feasible if he didn't have a huge mortgage tying him down.

Alec was only thirty years old and had been paying his mortgage since he was twenty-seven. If the biweekly plan knocked almost seven years off his repayment, he would be only fifty years old by the time his house was paid off. This sounded like a much better age to retire at than in his sixties. Without a $1,500 monthly mortgage commitment weighing him down, Alec would have more options. Early retirement might not be so implausible.

19

Always Pay Your Bills on Time

It *is* a big deal if you don't pay your bills on time. A sizeable factor in establishing good credit is your ability to pay your bills in a timely fashion. By being delinquent in your payments, you are not only hurting your credit history, you are also incurring late fees from the creditor. In the case of large payment obligations like your mortgage, the late fee could be a considerable amount, even several hundred dollars a month.

If you tend to receive late fees consistently, you could even add a line to your budget under expenses called "late fees." This expense category might turn out to be shockingly high if you add up all the monthly charges to your various accounts. Having such an expense category is counterproductive. This money is really wasted money. By being diverted to cover late fees, it cannot be used to pay off debts or add to your savings. Ironically, the people who can least afford to pay late fees are usually the ones who do. Living on the edge or over it makes late fees a certainty . . . maybe not every month but from time to time.

Some people have the mistaken notion that if they fall behind they can make a double payment the next month to catch up. A twenty-year-old foreign exchange student named Carlos told me that in his country this was standard practice. When he arrived at the University of Michigan, he just assumed the same rules were in effect.

Carlos spent his junior year at Michigan following this payment schedule. He would reliably miss a month and then make a double payment the next month. Since he never got more than two months behind, the creditors didn't call him to demand payment. They were assured by his payment history that he always caught up.

But what the creditors did carry out was the assessment of a penalty fee on his account for every payment that was late. However, Carlos didn't notice the fees because he never bothered to read his credit-card statements. He just zoomed in on the minimum payment due.

By not reviewing his statements closely, he also missed the fact that his payments were doing nothing to reduce his balance. After interest charges and late fees were imposed, his minimum payments only succeeded in keeping him in place, never moving forward and sometimes being pushed back. To his creditors Carlos was a very lucrative customer, since he ensured them money from interest, late fees, and sometimes overlimit penalties each and every month.

In addition to the fact that Carlos seemed to be stuck in perpetual debt, he was also creating a very negative credit history. His credit history showed that he was always delinquent in his payment pattern. Even though his double payments served to get his accounts current, they did not serve to erase his skipped payments. Since most creditors report monthly to the major credit bureaus, his record reflected a nonpayment for every month that Carlos skipped.

Carlos didn't realize the consequences of his negative credit history until he tried to finance a used car. His credit was so bad that the dealer gave him the worst possible terms for his loan, with an interest rate in excess of 30 percent. This fact did not concern Carlos, however, since he never paid attention to interest anyway. What did concern Carlos was the knowledge that his car could be repossessed if he got behind in his payments. Hopefully this will inspire Carlos to start making timely payments!

20

Resist Temptation

Advertising messages bombard us every day with "Buy this, buy that." In fact, a typical teenager will process more than three thousand discrete advertisements in a single day and 10 million by the time he or she is eighteen, according to *Merchants of Cool*, a PBS "Frontline" documentary. We are a consumer culture preaching consumption and accumulation of "stuff." Have you ever heard the saying "Whoever dies with the most stuff wins"? Comedian George Carlin even has a skit that talks about "stuff." He says, "The only reason we move to a larger house is because we have more stuff."

In addition to the subtle or not-so-subtle pressure we get from advertising, we are also confronted with peer pressure. In our desire to fit in, we want to appear hip. This may involve buying the latest styles in clothes, sunglasses, shoes, et cetera. Since styles change with the seasons, it becomes necessary to replenish our outdated wardrobe often. This can become quite an expensive task.

Additionally, we have the pressure we apply on ourselves from our own wants and desires. We may feel compelled to buy things that our budget has said "no" to but our compulsions say "yes." Regardless of the source of temptation, whether advertising, peer pressure, or self-imposed, the struggle to resist temptation is the same.

Darlene had a very difficult time resisting trips to the mall. Even though she was an attractive young woman of twenty-five, she never felt attractive inwardly. She tried to hide her insecurities through always dressing in the newest fashions. To maintain a current wardrobe in light of the constantly changing fashions, she visited the mall often.

This compulsion to always dress chic did not come cheap. Darlene habitually spent more each month on clothes than she did on rent. When she ran low on cash, she just charged things. Her shopping addiction was slowly becoming a mountain of debt that was too high to surmount. Something had to be done to curb her excessive spending.

Darlene, on advice from a friend, went to talk to a therapist about her spending addiction. After several sessions the therapist made a professional assessment that her spending addiction was just a symptom of her root problem, which was low self-esteem. So they started to work on building her self-confidence instead of dealing with her overspending tendencies.

This process did not provide Darlene with a quick fix, to her chagrin. Trying to overcome her lifelong feelings of inadequacy was not easy. But in time, Darlene did not feel such an intense need to visit the mall. She was learning to derive self-esteem from things other than her appearance.

Even though Darlene made great progress in her therapy sessions, she still was very weak whenever she found herself in the vicinity of a boutique, mall, or shoe store. To address this weakness, her therapist suggested she avoid any type of fashion establishment as much as possible. This compromise has worked well for Darlene. She still has a shopping spree from time to time, but it never wreaks serious havoc with her budget.

The struggle to resist temptation is not an easy one; therefore, we need to find ways to make it easy to say no. As Darlene learned, avoiding the source of temptation is one way. If you love shoes, avoid a shoe sale. If you are trying to lose weight, don't visit an ice cream parlor. If you have a gambling problem, avoid casinos.

You may choose to leave your credit cards behind when you shop and only carry the cash with you that you can afford to spend. When it is gone, you can spend no more. One woman even froze her credit cards in a block of ice. When she had the desire to go shopping, she would have to wait for the ice surrounding the cards to melt. During this waiting period, she normally talked herself out of her shopping urge. These resistance techniques and others can be extremely effective to counter the temptations to buy that surround us. Keep in mind, however, that the greater the urge, the more extreme the resistance measures that will be necessary.

21

Free Does Not
Always Mean Free

Is it possible for something that is initially free to end up costing you in the long run? It's hard to look beyond the immediate fact that you are getting something for nothing. But what might have no costs associated with it when you take possession of the item may turn out to be quite expensive down the road.

For instance, be wary if a friend offers you his or her used car for free. It might need serious mechanical work. Beware if someone gives you a used computer printer that eats up the paper each time you try to print a page. You might get an estimate to repair the printer only to discover you could buy a brand-new printer for less. Even if you adopt a dog for free from a shelter, the long-term costs of caring for the dog can be more than you had anticipated.

Melissa had always wanted a dog, so much so that in her apartment search she only visited complexes that allowed pets. After she found a place that she liked and put down her deposit, she promptly visited the animal shelter.

It was a hard decision, but Melissa finally settled on a cute little cairn terrier mix. The puppy was only eight weeks old and full of energy. As she filled out the paperwork to adopt the puppy that she decided to call Sandy, Melissa read in the contract that she needed to pay the shelter $80 to neuter the puppy. She hadn't anticipated this fee, but by now Melissa was so smitten by Sandy that there was no turning back.

Once Melissa's new landlord discovered she had a dog, Melissa was required to pay a pet deposit for any damage that might be done to the apartment. Melissa had also not anticipated this cost, but she had no choice. Soon these unplanned costs became a pattern.

Since Melissa's new job required her to travel frequently, a boarding kennel became Sandy's home away from home. Melissa found that the kennel costs started to become a significant monthly expense. She even tried to write off the costs as a business expense when she did her income taxes. Unfortunately, her accountant said that kennel costs were not an allowable deduction.

Next came the cost of dog training. Sandy had a habit of jumping up on Melissa whenever she arrived home. Sandy was probably just excited to see her after a long day, but the jumping was putting runs in Melissa's panty hose and ripping her business suits. In an effort to curb this behavior Melissa hired a dog trainer, who recommended an eight-week session. These private lessons did not come cheap. They did succeed in stopping the jumping—but they didn't keep Sandy from chewing on Melissa's Persian rug.

The first time that Melissa arrived home to see three quarter-sized holes chewed in her beautiful Persian rug, she started crying. She was certain that the rug was ruined. A friend told her not to worry, the rug could be fixed. Her friend was right, but the repair cost $400 . . . half the cost of the rug when she first bought it.

Destructive pet behavior can cause all kinds of damage to your personal property. Your dog could chew your furniture, pee on your rugs, or track mud into the house. This destruction can be rather expensive as you pay to repair damaged items or have your carpets cleaned.

Shortly after the rug incident, Melissa's neighbor Fred told her he was moving. This was sad news because she had become friends with Fred. She would miss him, but she would miss even more the fact that he walked Sandy each day at lunchtime. Fred worked out of his home and took a daily walk to get out of the apartment so he wouldn't go stir-crazy. He had offered to walk Sandy for free since he wanted the company. With Fred gone, Melissa had to hire a dog walker. This service also didn't come cheap.

On top of the expenses already mentioned, Melissa frequently bought dog toys, had Sandy groomed, and brought her for regular visits with the veterinarian. When Melissa first decided to adopt a dog, she had considered the costs of food but didn't really comprehend all the additional costs.

It is important to be aware of all the possible expenses (and compare them against your budget) before you make a decision to get something for free. You need to determine "How free is free?"

Try to figure out any related costs that may occur as a result of getting something for free. Are there maintenance costs? If the item is used, will there be repair costs? If you win a vacation, what costs are covered? The prize might be free airfare, but once you arrive you'll still have to pay for hotel, food, and entertainment costs on your own. Questions such as these need to be seriously considered before you accept anything for free. If you don't ask them, you may be stuck with expenses that may seem a surprise but should have been anticipated.

Livin' Large

22

Don't Try to Keep Up with the Joneses

Prosperity, of course, is a moving target. Most people are content if they make more money than their brother-in-law. And we all know about the Joneses. We try to keep up with them, but every time we get close, they refinance.

There will always be someone richer than you. There are those who are actually richer than you and those who just appear to be richer than you. Your colleagues, friends, and acquaintances might all seem financially prosperous. Their new cars, maid service, vacations overseas, tailored suits, and high-tech gadgets all seem to confirm your suspicions.

Beware of only seeing part of the entire picture. The missing information might change your mind. The credit-card debt surpassing their paychecks, the second mortgage secured to pay for their credit-card debt, and the collection phone calls are all invisible to a casual observer. Although your car may not be as new as theirs or your apartment as upgraded, your financial situation might be surprisingly superior. It is important to remember that looks can deceive.

One time I was returning from lunch to my office at Consumer Credit Counseling Service (CCCS) and I noticed a beautiful Jaguar pulling into the parking lot in front of me. The Jag parked next to me, and a man emerged wearing an expensive Italian suit with equally expensive shoes. I soon discovered that he was going to the same place that I was.

Unlike my work-related reason to be there, he was at CCCS to make a payment toward his debt management plan. Six months earlier he had escaped filing bankruptcy by electing to pay his debts through CCCS, who had worked out a repayment plan with his creditors. After he left, I asked the client representative to pull up his account and discovered that this man owed approximately $80,000 on numerous credit cards. In addition, he had secured a sizable second mortgage on his house, effectively canceling out any equity he might have had.

After many years of working in the credit-counseling field, this scenario no longer shocked me. Prior to entering the field, I used to take everything at face value. When I saw people who looked like they were wealthy, I assumed they were. But after becoming jaded from witnessing too many people with money troubles, I replaced this assumption with another. I no longer presumed that a wealthy-looking individual was rich; I just concluded that he or she was seriously in debt.

Your financial goals and plans need to be personal. They should be tailored to your situation alone and no one else's. When you stop comparing and contrasting, you effectively pull yourself out of the race to keep up with the Joneses. How can we expect an accountant to try to compete with a surgeon's salary or a tailor to compete with an aerospace engineer's? Similarly, if your investment goal is to earn 14 percent annually in the market and you realized a 16 percent growth, you shouldn't be concerned that your best friend saw his investments grow 18 percent.

Competing with the Joneses just leads to frustration and feelings of inadequacy. Wouldn't it be better to concentrate on your own situation and try to make it better? As long as your financial situation is improving instead of declining, you are making forward strides. If you consistently receive a salary increase or your overall net worth continues to rise, these are positive indicators that you are moving in the right direction. The sense of accomplishment that comes from improving your financial well-being should be the ultimate prize. But never forget that the race is a solitary one.

23

Be Willing to Give Up the Wants

If you spend more than you make or you spend every dime that you make, you will be unable to save any money. In order to make your financial situation better, you either need to increase your income or decrease your expenses. Increasing your income is usually the more difficult of the two.

Making more money at your current job is tough in the present climate of shrinking corporate profits and staff being downsized. Instead of negotiating for a large raise, you might just be happy that you have a job! And forget your reliable Christmas bonus . . . that may have been a thing of the past.

If you need to increase your salary considerably, you might need to work in a commission job (which comes with a certain degree of risk attached) or change companies in order to boost your pay. And let's not forget working overtime (if your company has not frozen overtime hours) or working an additional part-time job (which can be exhausting). Since the various avenues to increasing your income are challenging, it might be simpler to focus on reducing your expenses first.

Cutting back on your expenses should leave your "needs" intact while cutting down or eliminating your "wants." This is easier said than done. Giving things up is very difficult, especially if it involves expenses that are "fun" in nature. It is natural to resist giving up the cell phone, expensive hair salons, or your favorite chic restaurant.

This struggle to cut back plagued Jake almost every day. He had recently graduated with a master's degree in journalism from Northwestern University. Shortly after graduation, he found a job as a reporter with a small community newspaper just outside of Chicago. On his meager starting salary, he was barely able to pay his living expenses once his sizable student loans became due, six months after receiving his diploma. Jake hadn't realized how hefty these monthly payments would be. He had continued to apply for student loans each year with little thought about the total debt he was accumulating.

When the realization hit that his student loan payments were almost equal to his rent, he had already settled into a certain lifestyle. Although Jake's apartment was a small studio in a moderately priced neighborhood, he liked to go out with his college friends almost every weekend in Chicago. These weekends were costly after the bar tabs, expensive restaurants, and pricey nightclubs added up. His college buddies, who all seemed to be working as lawyers, financial analysts, or engineers, embraced this lifestyle.

With his new student loan obligations, Jake knew he wouldn't be able to continue his weekend spending at this level. But he couldn't figure out a way to tell his friends the news without humiliating himself. He felt like a loser because he couldn't keep up with them financially. He knew deep down that he was as smart and driven as they all were, but the difference was that he had chosen a profession that paid much less than theirs. In the end, Jake couldn't get up the nerve to be honest with his friends about his situation. He continued to join them every weekend and spend money he didn't have.

Jake's friends eventually discovered his financial predicament when he was evicted from his apartment. To Jake's surprise, they all rallied around him and chipped in to pay his share when they went out. They wanted his company more than they wanted his money. With such good friends, Jake was embarrassed that he hadn't come clean earlier.

Cutting back on our expenses involves choices. We either make these choices ourselves or they are made for us, as Jake discovered when he was evicted. The bottom line is that if there is not enough money to go around, something must go. Wouldn't you rather have the choice of what gets cut from your budget before your car lender, landlord, electric company, or phone company makes it for you?

Unfortunately, cutting back will always involve a certain amount of pain. Learn to accept the sacrifices that you'll need to make to improve your financial situation. It is comforting to keep in mind that these sacrifices need not be permanent. Once you are back on your feet, you may be able to add these expenses back into your budget. Be careful, however, that you don't re-create the situation that got you into trouble in the first place.

24

Don't Spend More than You Make

At the end of 2000, the average personal savings rate in the United States was a negative 0.1 percent. This meant that the average American couldn't save at all and was probably spending more than he or she was making. If we lived in a purely cash-based economy, this situation could not occur. However, since our system is heavily integrated with the borrowing of money, it is possible to spend more than you make.

Surprisingly, many people in this situation don't even realize it. Ellen was one such person. She had graduated from college a few years back and was now working as an administrative assistant for an association in Washington, D.C. Ellen knew that she had to start off in a low-level position since she had no serious work experience right out of college, unless you counted her waitress jobs. She was resigned to the fact that she needed to start off at the bottom, but she definitely didn't want to stay there.

If she worked hard and looked the part, she was confident she would get promoted soon. In order to "look the part," Ellen decided that she needed to dress well. She started expanding her wardrobe to include expensive business suits, shoes, and matching purses. These things did not come cheap.

Ellen didn't worry if she was short of cash; she just charged the purchases. She knew she was acquiring debt, but she told herself that when she received her promotion a large raise would come with it. Then she would be able to start paying down her credit cards. Now was the time to look good, whatever the price.

Well, the price turned out to be a steep one, as Ellen's promotion didn't come soon enough. She had succeeded in racking up so much debt that she was unable to make even the minimum credit-card payments after awhile. To make matters worse, another administrative assistant got the promotion that Ellen had coveted.

Since none of us has a crystal ball to foretell the future, it is better to live in the present. Our current situation is one that we are familiar with; it doesn't need a prediction. The salary we make now should be the basis for making our lifestyle choices. All of our spending and savings decisions should be influenced by our earned income, not by any supplemental income like cash advances from our credit cards.

In order to truly gauge if you are spending beyond your means, you need to accurately determine the balance between your income and your expenses. You will either discover that your income exceeds your expenses, the two are equal, or your income is less than your expenses. In the latter case, you have discovered that you are spending more than you make. This situation is never sustainable for a long time. You may succeed in using credit to cover the difference for a short time, but eventually you'll reach the limits of your creditworthiness.

25

Don't Spend Your Raise

As we make more money, we tend to also spend more money. As our salaries increase through job changes or promotions, our spending will usually increase as well. We usually try to expand our lifestyles alongside our salaries. Unfortunately, Megan found that she tended to live by that philosophy.

She was almost thirty years old and on her fourth job after college. She stayed an average of three years at each job and then moved on to a better opportunity. Megan found that she was able to increase her salary more by switching jobs instead of staying at the same company and hoping for a paltry raise each year.

Every time Megan started a new job, she told herself she wouldn't spend the increase in salary but instead would take the extra money each month and use it to pay off debts and start a savings account. This plan worked well in Megan's mind, but unfortunately it never translated into action. She always found some other way to spend her money.

One month she traded in her car for a better one. Megan justified this by saying that her old car was not reliable anymore and soon she would have to spend lots of money on repairs. The next month she bought a new winter coat and gave the used one to Goodwill. She insisted that after two seasons, it just wasn't in style anymore. Then she decided she needed more privacy, so she said goodbye to her roommate and rented her own apartment.

In the tug-of-war over her additional income, there was constant tension between the pull to get out of debt and the pull to fall in deeper. In Megan's case, the stronger of the two was the pull to spend her raise. Having extra money available was too tempting when she was confronted with the persuasiveness of advertising and peer pressure. Therefore, Megan never reduced her debt level or started saving. She just continued to spend every dime that she made.

It is much easier to expand our wants instead of cutting back on them. Even when we think we have everything we need, new inventions come along. There will always be new toys to replace the old. With this in mind, try not to spend your raise or any bonus you receive. Since you are not used to receiving this extra money, you won't miss it.

It would be better to invest the additional money. For example, if you are not contributing to your company's retirement plan you can start applying the extra money to the plan. Or if you are currently making contributions but not to the maximum amount allowed, you can contribute more. Finally, if you are one of those rare individuals who already contributes the maximum, you can use this extra money to pay down your debt or add to your individual retirement account (IRA or Roth IRA).

26

Don't Shop When You're Hungry

When you are starving, almost anything in the grocery store looks tasty. However, shopping while famished invariably causes you to buy more groceries. Since every aisle you walk down seems to have something that would taste good at the moment, you tend to throw more things in your cart. I've even found that I buy food that I don't really like when I'm hungry.

The hunger that requires food to be satisfied is not the only hunger that drives our actions. If you have been raised in poverty, you may hunger for wealth. In this instance, the starving you may have felt was not from lack of food but from the lack of physical comforts. This hunger can drive you to acquire expensive things in order to escape the deprivation of the past.

Antonio had just turned twenty-eight, but his memories of when he was a boy were very fresh. In fact, these memories governed most of his present actions. He grew up in a poor working-class neighborhood outside of New York City. From as far back as he could remember, he wanted to move away. His first job when he was a teenager was working nights as a bellboy for a luxury hotel in Manhattan.

This job put him in the company of the hotel's rich guests. Antonio liked being around them. He was impressed by the watches and clothes they wore and the briefcases and luggage they carried. Antonio started to develop exquisite tastes, but on his bellboy's salary he would have to be content to gaze instead of own.

His hunger for luxury steadily became stronger, along with his resolve that someday he would also own what they did. This need drove Antonio to study harder in school, and he eventually won a full scholarship to college. After he graduated, he went directly to law school. After earning his law degree and passing the New York bar exam, he started working for a law firm in Manhattan.

Over the years, Antonio became a workaholic—even by lawyers' standards. His obsessive work ethic was not for love of the work but for love of the money that resulted from the work. Regardless of the fact that he now made more money per hour than his father made in a week, he was not content.

The problem was that Antonio could never satisfy his hunger. The expensive items he bought did nothing to stop his hunger pangs. This was because his spending was a direct consequence of his feelings of low self-worth. As long as he believed he didn't belong among the "rich," no amount of lavish spending would change that belief.

In the same way, if you lack attention or affection, you may be starving for love. This hunger could drive you to spend money to try and buy love—through expensive gifts, exotic vacations, or fancy dinners out. But the old saying "You can't buy love" has been consistent in its wisdom throughout the years.

Whatever the source of the hunger, unless it is acknowledged your spending appetite will continue to be ravenous. Never forget that you *will* spend more if you shop when you are hungry.

27

Don't Spend Windfalls with Abandon

The tendency to believe that large sums of money received will last forever is quite common. If you have received an inheritance or won the lottery, you may think you couldn't possibly spend such a large amount. The windfall might be equal to several years' salary, and depositing it in the bank all at once can lead to illusions of wealth. Once your mindset becomes that of a "rich person," your whole philosophy toward money changes. As a "rich person," you may not feel the need to budget your money and control your spending because your funds are no longer limited. Your old habits of comparison shopping, clipping coupons, frequenting flea markets, and flying coach class are now considered irrelevant. These habits become supplanted with others more suitable for your new rich life, such as shopping at Gucci, dining at five-star restaurants, and flying first class.

Believe it or not, if you start to spend with abandon, even large sums of money can disappear very quickly. The old adage "Easy come, easy go" applies quite frequently if you engage in a spending spree. The speed with which you spend your windfall is determined by the cost of the items you decide to buy. The more expensive the items are, the faster the money will disappear.

Carla was only twenty-three years old when her father died from a heart attack. Her parents were divorced, so Carla and her sister, Mary, split their father's inheritance. However, the sisters handled their inheritance in completely opposite ways. Mary was the more conservative of the two and chose to put the vast majority of her inheritance in her savings account. Carla, on the other hand, was a liberal spender. She felt that she needed the money now more than later since she was young and just starting out.

Carla chose to use the money for a down payment on a condominium and a new car, which she bought with cash. After she moved into her condo she bought new furniture, appliances, and electronic equipment. Once her place was furnished, she then turned her attention to her wardrobe. Carla upgraded her taste in clothes to designer fashions. She preferred expensive clothes, and now that she could afford them she didn't see why she had to continue hunting for bargains or shopping only during sales.

Carla's share of the inheritance was approximately $80,000. This was an enormous sum for a recent college graduate who was only making $28,000 a year. To Carla, this money seemed unlimited. She could continue to buy everything she "needed" without worrying about the money running out. If Carla had kept track of her purchases, though, she wouldn't have been so cavalier in her worry-free attitude. Mary, out of concern over Carla's freewheeling spending, did a calculation of her sister's finances. Carla had already spent a total of $70,000 of her inheritance.

With only $10,000 left in the bank, Carla no longer felt that she had unlimited funds and put a rapid brake on her extravagant expenditures. Her mind-set immediately reverted back to that of a person with a lower income. She started budgeting again and weighed each purchase carefully before deciding to buy. She felt she needed to conserve to keep her remaining $10,000 from vanishing.

At least Carla still had money left when her financial situation was calculated. Many times the calculations are done only after the money is completely gone, leaving mortgages, car payments, and other large expenses vulnerable to nonpayment. Often these payments are only made possible by supplemental income from a windfall. Once the windfall is gone, so is the ability to meet your financial obligations.

Money that you work for has more value than money received with little effort attached. The effort of purchasing a winning lottery ticket, cashing a tax-refund check, or signing some inheritance papers hardly seems to warrant the money received in return. Conversely, your paychecks are directly related to your hard work. You vividly remember the hours spent working in order to get a paycheck. Understandably, it is not as easy to part with this money.

We should be just as careful with windfall money as we are with our paychecks. It's crucial that we learn to view these large windfall sums as money to last over a long period of time instead of over the short run. If you join the race to spend it as quickly as possible, the race may be an exhilarating one but the finish line is reached before you know it.

28

Live Below Your Means

Your income should dictate your lifestyle limitations. For instance, if you are a young recent college graduate, your aspirations may be high but your entry-level salary low. You may want a luxury apartment, new car, and designer clothes right now, but the reality of your situation says that you must wait.

However, it is possible to live a lifestyle that you can't afford. One common way to accomplish this is to use cash advances from your credit cards to supplement your income. This additional influx of cash works like a mirage. It seems like you have more money than you actually do.

Christopher didn't have much patience. He graduated with a degree in communications with a broadcasting concentration and was lucky enough to get a job as a production assistant at a local TV news station. Even though his job was more "glamorous" than most, his salary was certainly not something to write home about. Christopher understood that he had a coveted job, and he felt lucky to have it. He was certain that his salary would increase as soon as they made him anchor of the evening news.

Christopher's expectations were very unrealistic. Rarely does a young production assistant make the jump to news anchor without putting in many years of hard work at lower-level positions. Normally the move up the ladder also necessitates moving multiple times to progressively bigger and bigger markets.

In addition to being impatient, Christopher was also overly optimistic. He felt he would be "discovered" and then wouldn't have to put in all the years of paying his dues. His optimism was substantiated by his promotion to weekend sports announcer. Although this new position increased his visibility since he was now in front of the camera and not behind it, his salary increased only slightly.

Christopher was not deterred by anything in his quest to become the show's anchor. He decided that if he could visualize it then it would happen. He not only pictured himself as the anchor in his mind, he started to act and dress the part as well. He acquired many new suits and bought a new sports car (appropriate for his job as a sports reporter). The fact that the show's other personalities routinely wore suit jackets with jeans below the waist did not stop him from wearing a full suit along with expensive shoes.

This odd mixing of attire was adopted primarily because the salary of a local news reporter was not enough to buy both the top and the bottom of an outfit. Adding expensive shoes to the mix was an impossibility. Since the area from the waist down was not seen by TV viewers, the obvious assumption was that the complete suit was being worn. But it was only in Christopher's case that this assumption was correct.

Unfortunately for Christopher, the consequence of trying to look as well as act the part was putting him deeper in debt. His meager salary would not have allowed him to purchase all the business suits that were now part of his wardrobe. With his new high car payment added to his rent, he barely had money left over each month for food and other essentials. It was only thanks to his many credit cards that he was able to buy clothes and shoes.

His gradual accumulation of debt finally reached a level where he could no longer make even the minimum payments on his credit cards. He didn't know what to do until by chance one day the news show featured a story on debt. Their guest was from a nonprofit credit-counseling agency. Christopher called and made an appointment to see a counselor as soon as the show was over.

Christopher arrived incognito (wearing a hat and dark glasses) because he was embarrassed to be seen in the lobby. Just his luck, he was seen by the same counselor who had been the guest on the show. The counselor saw through Christopher's disguise and assured him that his secret was safe with her. In fact, the counselor shared that she regularly saw local celebrities such as school superintendents, elected officials, and newscasters. She explained that debt does not discriminate between the rich, the poor, or the famous. If they spend more than they make, they are all in debt.

Unlike your paycheck, credit is not your money. If you mistakenly treat it as such, you can easily believe that your income is inflated. But if you spend more than you make, it will eventually catch up to you. Living below your means requires making tough decisions about expenses that need to be cut back or expectations that need to be scaled down. But by not living within your means, indebtedness is a certainty.

29

Get an Advanced Education

The reality is that increased education and increased pay go hand-in-hand. The statistics show that the higher the educational level you attain, the higher the salary you will command. A "diploma premium" is attached to each advanced educational level. Even though these statistics are indisputable, many recent high-school graduates opt to choose work over an advanced education.

The justifications may make this decision seem like a very wise move. A high-paying job, which would seem foolish to pass up, may be awaiting the recent graduate. Or the cost of college may seem too daunting to afford. However, what may seem a wise money decision for the immediate future may not be wise for the more distant (but long-term) future.

Kenny had been an athlete all through high school. In fact, he was a starter on the school's football and baseball teams. His part-time job during high school was at a local health club. He had been working there since he was sixteen years old. He started doing menial tasks like collecting dirty towels. He then graduated to working the front reception desk and then to assisting the personal trainers. By his senior year, Kenny had been promoted to membership salesperson. This turned out to be an area in which he excelled. His sales record rivaled that of the full-time employees even though he worked part-time.

As graduation was nearing and Kenny pondered applying to a local community college, his health club gave him a very generous offer. They were opening a new location and they wanted Kenny to be one of their head salesmen. The commission structure they outlined for him was very lucrative. In addition, because the location was new the memberships would initially be at a higher volume than a club that already had an established member base.

To Kenny, the decision between joining the working world or going to college was an easy one. On the one hand, he had a potentially high salary for a recent high-school graduate. Kenny was already dreaming about the car he would buy with all the money he was going to make. He would also have freedom since he would be able to afford to move out of his parents' home.

His other option was much less appealing. He would face years of homework, tests, and term papers. He would be stuck living at home with his parents and have a large student loan to pay off upon graduation. Not to mention the fact that his spending money would be limited by the hours he would be able to work around his class schedule.

Kenny's ultimate decision to choose work over school was one that he did not regret for the first year. As the health club's membership expanded, so did his wallet. Unfortunately, as the second year progressed, his fortunes did not continue their rapid increase as they did the first year. As the club's membership base hit a plateau, his commissions leveled off and became steady but not highly profitable. He started to receive a more "normal" salary typical of his industry.

Many of Kenny's friends who had chosen to go on to college came home for the summer break and shared with him their college experiences and their envisioned career plans. Several had decided to get business degrees, others were pursuing degrees in marketing, and one friend had decided to go on to law school. They all seemed to be very hopeful about their future and their income potential.

Kenny started to regret his decision not to go to college. His future income prospects looked to be similar to what he was making right now. Unless he became a manager of the health club or was willing to relocate to open a new club, he couldn't imagine his salary increasing dramatically. He would have to be content with his current standard of living.

Kenny's choice to reject college left him with limited opportunities. This revelation caused him to rethink the wisdom of not getting a college degree. Eventually he started applying to colleges, deciding that "late is better than never."

The average salary of someone with a master's degree is double that of someone with only a high-school diploma. When a professional degree is attained, the person's salary will average four times more than that of a high-school graduate. (A professional degree is any degree beyond a master's. It could be a Ph.D., or for some fields, like architecture or dentistry, a special license.) Even when you factor in the costs associated with an advanced degree (tuition, room and board, textbooks, et cetera), the average lifetime earnings of college graduates are still far ahead of those who never pursued additional education after high school.

30

Defer Gratification

Many young adults who are just starting out expect to have everything their parents have without delay. For example, their first apartment needs to look exactly like their parents' home that they just left. Although arriving in an empty, unfurnished apartment is quite a shock after having left a fully furnished home, it is unrealistic to expect to acquire overnight the furnishings that your parents spent many years accumulating.

Your parents probably started out with used furniture or hand-me-downs from their parents. But because it is easier to access credit at a younger age than ever before, it is possible for young adults to visit a home-furnishings store and get an immediate line of credit. This extension of credit will allow them to get a lot of new "stuff." No more need to suffer with used, damaged, or (heaven forbid) out-of-style furniture when new stuff is so easily acquired. Unfortunately, this stuff comes with a hefty price tag after you calculate the added interest.

Initially Janelle had no intention to purchase lots of furniture when she entered The Ultimate Furniture Store. She was on a mission only to find a dresser for her clothes. Once she located an acceptable dresser, she had accomplished her task. Since the cashier was located in the far back corner of the store, it was necessary to pass through the bedroom, living room, kitchen, and bathroom departments on her way.

Janelle had planned on paying for the dresser with money that she had saved. The cashier informed her, however, that she could fill out a credit application and qualify for up to $5,000 in credit on the spot. She encouraged Janelle to take five minutes and complete the application because that was the only way she would be able to receive a 10 percent discount on her purchase.

Janelle thought it would be foolish to pass up any chance to save money so she took the five minutes. As she was completing the application, her furniture-buying expectations were suddenly broadened. Why buy only a dresser if she could qualify for $5,000 worth of additional furniture? She did need a better couch to replace her old worn one. Why miss this opportunity?

Janelle settled on a new white leather couch. After it was delivered it almost filled up her entire small living room. But what a statement it made when her friends came over to visit. Almost everyone commented on how they wished they could afford a couch like hers.

When Janelle's best friend, Amy, went on a vacation for a week, she asked Janelle to take care of her German shepherd while she was away. Janelle liked the dog, Arnold, so she agreed. Amy assured her that Arnold was housebroken and wouldn't be any trouble.

To Janelle's horror, she arrived home from work the first day to discover her new couch totally destroyed. Arnold had chewed the wooden legs and had succeeded in ripping holes in the leather and pulling out most of the stuffing. The couch was beyond repair; it would have to be replaced.

When Amy returned from her trip, she was very apologetic but unable on her low salary to pay for a replacement. Besides, she had charged over $1,200 on her credit cards for her vacation since she had no savings. Janelle was left with no choice but to buy another couch on her own. To make matters worse, she still owed money on her destroyed leather couch. In fact, her monthly payments were so low that she still had two more years left to pay off the balance. Not only did she have to pay for another couch, but she was stuck making payments on a couch that was no longer in her possession.

If immediate gratification can be deferred, purchases bought on credit could instead be bought on cash. If time were taken to save up for a purchase instead of just financing it, the cost of the item in the long run would be dramatically lower. Buying with cash involves patience; but the price of patience is well worth the wait.

31

Don't Leave Home Too Soon

The desire to leave the nest can be quite strong. It is normal for young adults to want to assert their independence. They challenge curfews, ignore parental restrictions on who they can hang out with, and resist other household rules. Living on their own becomes the ultimate way to defy authority. But if they are not prepared for the financial realities of the marketplace, they may falter and end up moving back to the nest.

Doug did not plan his so-called "liberation" very well. He was guided exclusively by a need for speed. Doug couldn't wait to move out from under the iron fist of his parents, who regulated every aspect of his life . . . or so it seemed. This speediness caused him to rent the first place he visited that was in his price range.

Doug's excitement about moving resulted in tunnel vision. He only saw from door to door and nothing in-between. If his peripheral vision were working, he would have seen that his new neighborhood was in a crime-ridden area of town and that his complex's parking was not secure. There was no security fence surrounding it like many of the other complexes in the area.

Doug only noticed that this important amenity was missing after his car was. While walking to his car one morning on his way to work, Doug realized that it was gone. At first he thought he had just parked it in another space, but upon frantic inspection it was nowhere to be found. Someone had indeed stolen it.

This unfortunate incident was ill-timed in so many ways. First it caused the dilemma of how to get to and from work. Doug's job was a forty-five-minute drive away, which turned into a two-hour commute when he was forced to take the bus. He had to make changes to two different lines along the way. Carpooling was not an option since no one at his company lived close to his crime-ridden neighborhood. Doug was forced to buy another car to make his commute manageable.

The second ill-timed result of the robbery was that Doug had just cancelled his car insurance in order to have enough money for rent. Therefore, he didn't receive a settlement from the insurance company to help him replace the car. He was forced to come up with his own down payment. This car purchase ended up wiping out his savings account.

The last ill-timed consequence was that he was laid off at his job. It didn't have anything to do with his performance. Doug was the victim of more bad timing. Since he was the youngest employee and the most recently hired, he was the first to go. His company had three straight quarters of losses and they were forced to cut costs. Personnel was their greatest expense.

With no income and no savings, Doug quickly had trouble paying his rent and car payment. Before he knew it, he was several months behind on both. Not to mention that he had no money to buy food. The only solution he could come up with was one that was unbearable—move back in with his parents.

Young adults who find themselves back home after being out on their own may have a hard time adjusting to the loss of freedom. It can also be a difficult adjustment for parents, who might have been enjoying their peace and quiet. In order to avoid this disruptive reverse migration back to the nest, young adults need to be financially prepared before they leave home in the first place.

Doing a "moving-out" budget is a must. This entails figuring out the lifestyle you can afford. Since rent is usually the largest item in your budget, a simple calculation is essential. First you determine how much money equals 30 percent of your net income. Your rent payment should not exceed this amount. For example, if you make $2,000 a month after taxes, your rent should not exceed $600 a month. If you don't do this calculation in advance, you might end up in an apartment you can't afford.

A budget is not complete without subtracting other estimated living expenses like food, car payment, clothes, entertainment, utilities, and gas from your salary. The bottom line will show you the reality of your situation. You will either make more than you spend, spend more than you make, or spend as much as you make. The goal should be to always make more than you spend.

It's also crucial to estimate "moving-in" costs. These are one-time costs that many young adults don't know to factor in (first and last month's rent, deposits for opening utilities accounts, and phone hookup charges). Prospective renters may also be required to pay for their credit checks before they are approved. Landlords may even charge an extra deposit if you have a pet.

The final preparation before leaving the nest should be to accumulate savings. If you can save up a cushion of three to six months' worth of estimated expenses, you will be better prepared to handle the financial crises that are part of everyday life. If Doug hadn't been living so close to the edge, he probably would have been able to use his savings to pay for his expenses until he found another job. The drastic measure of moving back home wouldn't have been necessary.

32

Keep Personal Staff to a Minimum

The old saying "Time is money" is very relevant in today's busy world. Americans now work more hours on average than even the traditionally hardworking Japanese. Since we have less free time, this time becomes precious. If our limited free time becomes disproportionately filled with yard work and cleaning the house, we may start to feel resentful that we have no time for "fun." The simple answer to freeing up more time is to hire others to do these tasks for you by employing maid services, lawn services, dog walkers, pool cleaners, baby-sitters, and laundry services.

In addition to household jobs, there is a myriad of other personal services that can be performed by others. Do you bring your car to a car wash when you have the facilities to wash it yourself? Do you get professional manicures and/or pedicures? What about visiting a tanning booth?

Consider the case of Emily. Even though her income was not very high, Emily, twenty-five years old, was still making a decent income considering she had no children or husband to support. But when I saw her expenses, I understood why she was struggling financially. She took advantage of every possible service that others can do for you. Emily had someone wash her car and her dog, clean her house, give her a manicure and a pedicure, a facial, a massage, do her laundry, give her personal training at the gym, and so on.

The obvious solution to her financial dilemma was to perform these services herself and add the money saved back into her budget. Since her spending habits resulted in a huge percentage of her money going to pay "personal staff," the substitution of her "time" in place of her "money" would solve her money troubles.

From Emily's point of view that wasn't possible. For example, she said she couldn't wash her car herself because she didn't have the time. It would entail driving to the basement of her apartment complex to use the community hose. In addition, she would have to carry towels and shampoo needed for the car wash to the basement also.

Emily felt the whole process would be a waste of her precious time. In actuality, Emily regularly waited in long lines at the car wash. The time she spent waiting was probably equal or greater to the time it would have taken to do it herself.

All kinds of other excuses abounded. Emily needed weekly massages because her job was so stressful. The facials and manicures were necessary to maintain her professional decorum at work. The personal trainer was imperative because she didn't have the discipline to exercise on her own. Emily's insistence on keeping "personal staff" was blocking any possibility of her having a financial recovery.

You may feel it's worth the money to have lots of personal staff, but have you added up the actual expense? An eye-opening exercise is to make a list of all the services that you currently pay for that you could do yourself (if you had to). Once all these services are totaled up, you may be shocked by their combined cost.

If you are trying to keep your expenses to a minimum, you might want to consider trading a little more of your free time for keeping a little more of your money. Keep in mind that receiving some services may actually be more time-consuming than doing them yourself, if you have to wait in line or take time off work. It comes down to a matter of priorities. Is your time or your money more important? If you decide your priority is time, then make sure you have the financial means to afford personal staff before you start employing them.

Credit: It's Not Your Money

33

Never Have More than Two Credit Cards

The average American has nine credit cards. If you took out your wallet and counted, would you be below or above the average? Make sure you count every card, whether it's a gasoline, department store, retail store, or major credit card. If they are used to purchase items with money that is not yours, then they should be counted.

If you are surprised at how many credit cards you actually have, think back to how many times you took advantage of an offer to open an account today and receive 10 percent or 20 percent off your immediate purchases. You may have thought this was a smart financial move. Besides, you did not plan on using that credit card ever again—after you paid off the initial purchases. Did you end up sticking to that plan, or have you kept that card in your wallet and continued to make subsequent purchases with it?

Let's examine the case of Audrey, a twenty-five-year-old woman who received her first credit card when she was eighteen and working at a local department store. The department store had a policy that she could not receive her employee discount unless she bought her purchases with a department-store credit card.

Audrey was amazed at how easy it was to obtain additional credit cards after she had her first. The offers kept coming steadily, and when she started college they increased and became a deluge. In fact, on her first trip to the college bookstore she was given several credit card applications in her book bag. It didn't help that every day on the way to class she passed by the student union, which always seemed to have numerous credit-card displays. All that she had to do was fill out an application and she would get some cool giveaway.

The temptation of what Audrey saw as "free money" was too much for her to resist. Besides, how was she supposed to pay for the "fun" things in college if she didn't use her credit cards? This creative financing lasted until Audrey's junior year, when she found herself unable to pay even the minimum payment on her fifteen credit cards. When she tried to get a sixteenth card, she was turned down because delinquencies on her other accounts had started to show up on her credit report.

Unable to catch up on her own since she only worked weekends as a waitress, Audrey called her parents for help. At first they considered bailing her out, but they had no idea of the extent of her debt. After adding up Audrey's total debt, they were shocked by the fact that she owed $15,000! Her parents couldn't afford to pay that much, so Audrey was left with the options of filing bankruptcy or dropping out of school to work full-time and pay her debts. She chose to file bankruptcy and joined the 4 percent of total filers who are aged twenty-five and under.

Audrey could have avoided this situation if she had only followed my two-credit-card rule. This rule works under the premise that the more credit cards you have, the more you will charge. By keeping the maximum number of credit cards in your possession to two, you will limit the debt you could accumulate. If Audrey had stuck to only two cards, she would have limited her debt load to a manageable one. An important caveat is that your two credit cards should also have relatively low limits. If you have two credit cards with credit lines of $10,000 you can also get into trouble.

There is a mistaken notion that you need lots of credit cards to build a credit history. This notion is false. You only need one or two that you pay on time and preferably in full every month. As Ann Landers once said, "The easiest way to get a fatter wallet is to take out your credit cards!"

34

Know Your Debt Level

Most Americans have no idea how much they owe. They might have a vague notion of the amount, but when they actually add it up they have usually underestimated the extent of their debt. This was the case for a young couple, Anna and Martin, who had recently married. Prior to their marriage they had to enroll in a premarital counseling course at their church. During this course, their finances were discussed.

Anna felt relieved when Martin disclosed that he owed only around $3,000. Anna had seen debt problems plague her parents' marriage and didn't want to relive their troubles in her own marriage. It wasn't until Anna started paying the couple's bills for the first time that she noticed a large discrepancy. Martin's debt was not the $3,000 he had revealed—when added up it was closer to $8,000. When she confronted him with this bombshell, Martin was genuinely surprised.

Martin said that he hadn't realized the total amount of his debt since he paid only the minimum payment on each of his eight credit cards. Since many creditors only asked for a minimum payment equal to 2 to 3 percent of his total outstanding amount, he was used to paying only $40 on a $2,000 balance. His small monthly payments coupled with the fact that Martin never read his statements (he only looked at the minimum amount due) ensured that he never realized the total amount of his debt.

Although Anna was not legally responsible for any of the debts that Martin had accumulated prior to the marriage, the consequences of his debt became a concern for both of them. Instead of being able to put extra money away each month in a savings account, they now used any additional funds to pay down Martin's debt. Anna started to feel resentful that part of her hard-earned income was being used to pay off credit-card expenditures that she had not benefited from. In fact, Anna ironically realized that she was probably helping to pay off dinners out and entertainment for Martin and his old girlfriend.

It wasn't until Anna started fighting with Martin over the fact that they had to postpone starting a family until they could afford it that she realized she had re-created her parents' situation. She had so desperately wanted to escape fighting over money, and that was exactly what she was now doing. Anna was so frightened by the prospect of following in her parents' footsteps that she insisted upon marriage counseling. Hopefully, this will solve their marital problems if not their financial ones.

Why is it so important to know how much you owe? For the simple reason that until you understand your actual situation, you may be living in a fantasy land and not reality. If you assume your debt level is manageable and in fact it is not, you won't see the need to take steps to curb your spending. The first step to reducing and ultimately eliminating your debt level is to know the bottom line. Your actual debt level might be incredibly frightening, but fear can be an incredible motivator.

35

Check Your Credit Report Regularly

It has been estimated that over 50 percent of credit reports contain some type of error. By checking your credit report on a regular basis, you can discover any errors before they seriously affect your potential to acquire additional credit or even prevent you from getting a job.

Credit reports are very powerful. They are being relied upon more and more to assess whether a lender should grant you credit, give you life insurance, or qualify you for a security clearance. Without such a clearance, many candidates are rejected for jobs in banks, branches of the military, or aerospace firms. All of these decisions are important ones since they radically impact your immediate and future goals. With the gravity of these reports in mind, it is essential to make sure that they are error-free.

Errors may include incorrect reporting of your payment history by indicating that a payment was late when it was actually on time, or that you failed to pay off an account when in fact you paid it in full. Other errors could be less serious, like not listing your updated address or place of employment. However, you may discover that there are extremely serious errors like an unauthorized individual using credit cards in your name or someone buying your social security number and committing identity theft.

Victoria, a college student at the University of Southern California, became a victim of credit fraud by a "dumpster diver" at her apartment's trash bin. Victoria unwittingly did what many of us do—she threw away her credit-card applications without even opening the envelopes. She had received so many of these applications since starting college that they were becoming not only an annoyance but also tempting. She wanted to get rid of them as soon as possible before she filled one out.

The dumpster diver, as the perpetrators are called since they rummage through people's garbage, simply picked her envelopes out of the trash. She then filled in the application with her own address and Victoria's name. When the card was issued in Victoria's name, it arrived at the con artist's home and was promptly used by her but signed with Victoria's name.

Victoria didn't discover this on her own. She received a phone call one evening from one of the credit-card companies for nonpayment on her account. It was only then that she was alerted to the fraud that was occurring. The company was able to "red-flag" her card and surprisingly caught the con artist when she went to use the card in Victoria's name. The store was alerted to the fraud being committed and called the police. From that moment on, Victoria always cut up her credit-card applications. This is a habit that everyone should adopt; it will put "dumpster divers" out of business.

If an inaccuracy in your credit report is a true mistake, you can contact the credit-reporting agency to dispute the entry in order to have it removed. If their research discovers that the error is in fact an error, they must correct your report. By law, any information that is not valid must be removed. It is vitally important that any illegal transactions be reported and the difficult process initiated to clear this fraudulent information from your credit report.

The sooner these errors can be discovered, the less damage will be done. This is why it is important to check your credit report regularly. The three major credit bureaus—Trans Union, Equifax, and Experian—charge only a nominal fee to do so. They contain similar but not identical information, so it is a good idea to check them all.

If this advice is not urgent now, it should become a major priority before any major purchase or job interview. Do yourself a favor and find out in advance what your future lender or employer is going to see. This knowledge may prevent any unwelcome surprises.

36

When You Pay with Credit and Are Reimbursed with Cash, Run to the Bank

Have you ever gone out to dinner with others and discovered, when it came time to pay the bill, that you didn't have enough cash to pay your portion? Probably. Did you then offer to put the entire bill on your credit card and ask the other members of the party to give you cash for their share? Probably. Did you then run to the bank and deposit the cash? Probably not. You most likely spent the cash instead of saving it.

By leaving this dinner money in your wallet you are suddenly flush with cash. Remember the advice from Chapter 13—don't carry lots of cash around with you. If you do, you will almost certainly spend more. And you can guarantee that when your credit card bill arrives, the dinner money will have been spent.

The same philosophy applies for business travel reimbursements. Susan, a twenty-five-year-old Los Angeles resident, worked as a consultant. This job required her to travel during the week and fly home for the weekends. All this time on the road put her credit card into overdrive as she charged plane trips, hotel rooms, rental cars, and meals out. Fortunately for Susan, her company was quick in reimbursing her.

Her expense checks were usually worth at least several thousand dollars. This caused her checking account to have an inflated balance. When it came time to pay her mortgage and other large bills, Susan would confidently write the checks, knowing she had plenty of money in her account to cover her bills. Unfortunately, by the time her credit-card statements—which contained her already-reimbursed business expenses—arrived, she had spent the repayment on other things like her mortgage and car payment.

The only reason Susan managed to pay her credit card bills on time was the fact that she continually received reimbursement checks. She then used the checks that coincided with not-yet-received credit card statements to pay her current charges. This worked until Susan's travel was put on hold after the September 11 World Trade Center terrorist attack.

It was then that Susan finally realized how behind she had become. She had advanced herself almost $4,000 of her company's money to pay her own expenses. Unable to rely on any reimbursements to arrive soon to cover her shortfall, Susan got a cash advance from one credit card in order to make the payment on the other. This enabled her to continue her cycle of borrowing. She just replaced one source of funds with another.

Whether you receive an advance reimbursement from your friends or your company, the result is the receipt of extra cash. This padded balance might lead to the misperception that this money is yours to use for your mortgage payment and other personal bills. But by depleting your account of these funds, when the credit card bill arrives, the money from the reimbursement will be long gone.

Mingling reimbursements with your own money can be confusing at best and lead to overspending at worst. The best way to avoid this situation is to separate reimbursements from your personal funds. Opening another account purely for deposit of business expense checks is an excellent way to ensure that the money will be there when the credit card bill arrives. This account should *never* be touched for your personal expenses. Similarly, when you receive money from your friends to cover expenses you have charged for them, make sure you run to the bank.

37

Never Get a Car Loan for Longer than Three Years

If the payments are stretched out long enough, anyone can afford a luxury car. A seven-year car loan is not unheard of. By the time a loan like this is paid off, the added interest has substantially increased the total cost of the car. In some cases, two cars could have been bought for the same price if you had only paid cash.

The reason most people give for choosing the longer loan term is that they couldn't afford the higher monthly payments for the shorter period. This turned out to be the case for David, a twenty-three-year-old electronics salesman who had his heart set on a new sports car, preferably a convertible. He decided to go to CarMax so he would have a large variety of cars to choose from. Once there, however, David felt overwhelmed by his options.

A salesman quickly appeared to help David navigate through the assortment of vehicles parked in the vast lot. David let the salesman know of his preference for a sports car and was guided to that area of the lot. Many of the vehicles that he saw there fit his vision of his dream car. The price in the window, on the other hand, didn't fit his pocketbook. David was told not to worry about the price; the salesman assured him that they would be able to work out the financing.

With price not being an object, David proceeded to select the car with the most features. He chose a red convertible that was fully loaded. It had leather seats, power windows, a CD player, cruise control, top-of-the-line speakers, and a navigation system. Why shouldn't he have a comfortable car, he said to himself, since he lived in Los Angeles and spent many hours each day stuck in traffic.

Once the car was chosen, David and the salesman went into the office to do the paperwork. Fortunately, David's credit report showed a positive credit history. He had always paid his bills on time and didn't carry much credit card debt. Because of this, he was able to get approved for a lower interest rate. His record of stable employment at the same company for the past two years also helped to ensure his approval.

David couldn't believe how smoothly the loan process was going. It wasn't long before the salesman showed him the terms of the loan. David was shocked at the number that was written on the "monthly payment" line . . . $700! This was more than what he paid in rent for the apartment he shared with a roommate.

There was no way that he could afford such a high car payment on his limited income. David's paycheck consisted of a meager regular salary supplemented by a commission that fluctuated radically from month to month, depending on how well his sales were going. This resulted in his income being unreliable. David compensated by trying to live on the consistent salary and not expecting the commissions to arrive.

This prudent money-management technique was not used as the basis for the salesman's figures, however. He calculated David's monthly income based on his yearly income divided by twelve. He presented the case to David that he could in fact afford the $700 payment. Even if he was right, David felt very uncomfortable agreeing to such a hefty payment.

His reluctance to commit to the deal caused the salesman to become more creative in his financing. He pulled out his calculator and worked out two alternate payment plan options. One option reduced the car payment to $500 a month and the other to $350. It was this last option that David finally agreed to.

David didn't seem concerned that the reason the payment was so low was because it required a seven-year loan commitment. He had no idea that the added interest would total approximately $8,400 after he finally paid off the car seven long years down the road.

David also didn't realize that if he decided to sell the car before the end of the loan period, he would probably be "upside down"—that is, he would owe more on the loan than he would be able to collect from the sale of the car, causing a shortage. This would be a result of his slow rate of paying down his loan. With only $250 each month going toward paying down the principal, the remaining $100 of his payment went toward interest. The rate of depreciation in the value of the car would surpass the rate at which he paid down his loan.

My advice is simple: if you can't afford the monthly payments for a car loan of three years or less in length, you simply can't afford that particular car. Choose another vehicle that is within the price range your budget can handle. By limiting the loan period to three years maximum, you will end up having a greater percentage of your monthly payment going toward the principal instead of toward interest. This will result in a huge savings in interest costs over the length of your loan.

38

Never Go to a Rent-to-own Store

If you don't have a credit history or you have a negative history, you may find you are turned down for credit when you apply for certain loans. If your poor credit history is disenfranchising you from the traditional credit market, you may choose rent-to-own stores as an alternative. The lure of low weekly payments can be very enticing. However, the interest rate charged at many of these stores can be so high that by the time you've paid for your TV set, you could have bought several TV sets if you had paid cash instead.

Lance learned the meaning of a credit report the hard way. Neither his parents nor his school had explained to him the importance of paying his bills on time or at all. So, he frequently skipped paying some months and just caught up the next month with a double payment. Since he eventually paid, what did consistency matter? He was twenty-one years old and had been following this pattern ever since getting his first bill at the age of eighteen. With this approach to bill-paying, it was no surprise that Lance's credit report had negative entries (late payments) for almost every account.

Now Lance wanted a television set but wasn't willing to wait until he had saved up enough money to purchase one. In order to get it immediately, he had to buy one on credit. This was proving difficult because his credit report was not portraying him as a good risk to the stores that decided whether to approve his application. After five stores had turned him down, Lance saw a sign in a rent-to-own store window promising

"Bad Credit, No Credit . . . No One Is Turned Away." The lure of low weekly payments was also very tempting. Lance went in and left soon afterwards carrying his brand-new television.

Lance felt he had made a wise decision. He got his television set without waiting, and he only had to make a small payment of $9.99 each week. Ironically, the next week Lance had a lesson in his college finance class that illustrated the total cost of his purchase. If Lance's repayment terms were extended to eighteen months, by the time he paid off his $220 television, he would have spent $800 with the additional interest charges. In fact, if he had read the small print on his contract, he would have discovered that the interest rate was 300 percent!

Most people, however, don't have the advantage of seeing the big picture. By only focusing on the $9.99 a week, it is easy to fool yourself into thinking that you have entered into a "good deal." Most rent-to-own stores assume that the average customer doesn't understand the cost of interest. In fact, they are probably betting on it.

Try waiting until you save enough money to purchase an item with cash instead of purchasing it immediately on credit. Our need for immediate gratification is what gets us into debt. It is a trade-off between time and money. Would you rather sacrifice time and wait longer but pay less, or sacrifice money and wait less but pay more? The choice is yours.

39

Get a Debt Consolidation Loan only If You follow These Rules

Debt consolidation loans can appear very attractive. If you are an average American with nine credit cards, bill paying is a time-consuming task. Nine checks need to be written, nine entries made in your checkbook (this assumes you are balancing your checkbook), and nine envelopes need to be addressed and stamped.

If you are like my friend Mario, who had twenty-three credit cards, it takes several hours each time you sit down to pay bills. In addition to going through the steps just listed, Mario's bill paying had an added layer of complexity because he didn't have enough money to go around. This necessitated his use of what I call "creative accounting."

This accounting method involved Mario frequently having to pay bills late in order to wait for an additional paycheck to hit his bank account. Other times he had to pay for one credit card with a check drawn on the funds of another credit card. Mario was elated whenever he received these credit card "checks" in the mail. The checks enabled him to tap an additional source of money much more easily than going to the bank and getting a cash advance on his credit card. It accomplished the same thing with minimal effort—all he had to do was sign the check. He used to wait in long lines at the bank to get cash advances, and that transaction alone usually took at least ten minutes to complete because it needed manager approval.

After a while Mario increasingly dreaded this time, which he considered not only wasted but also highly stressful. He eventually ran out of creative accounting solutions when he could no longer rob Peter to pay Paul. After he had reached his credit card limits, there was no one left to rob. Luckily, an alternate solution appeared on TV late one night while Mario was wide awake and worrying how to pay his bills.

The commercial was for a debt-consolidation loan company. In fact, it seemed that all the advertisements in the middle of the night were for debt-consolidation loans. "Financial worries must be a huge cause of insomnia," Mario pondered.

Despite his initial reservations, the prospect of mingling all his separate credit obligations into one loan with a lower interest rate seemed like a wise money strategy. Most appealing was the idea of reducing the number of checks he wrote each month from twenty-three to one. Mario was right in his assumption that debt-consolidation loans can be wise, but only if they are done correctly.

Unfortunately, Mario followed a common "unwise" debt-consolidation pattern. He started by paying off his numerous individual credit cards with the money from the loan provided by the debt-consolidation company. These separate balances were then consolidated into one large credit balance. After transferring the balances owed, Mario's credit cards now had zero balances.

The temptation of having "empty" credit cards was too much for Mario's overspending tendencies, which had gotten him into trouble in the first place. In a short time, he had charged them all to the max again. This resulted in double debt—the original debt that had been transferred to the debt-consolidation loan in addition to the newly acquired debt.

The best way for Mario to avoid this situation would have been to cut up his credit cards and close the accounts after the balances were transferred. This step is crucial because it prevents the accumulation of additional debt. If there is easy access to lines of credit through newly paid-off credit cards, additional debt buildup becomes inevitable for most people.

Another unintended consequence of unwise debt consolidation (in addition to debt-consolidation loans creating "double debt") is the fact that you may have turned an "unsecured" loan into a "secured" one. If your debt-consolidation loan is actually a home-equity loan, your house is in danger of foreclosure if you are unable to make payments. On the other hand, with unsecured credit-card debt, the probability of Master-Card coming into your home and seizing the clothes you charged and never paid for is extremely remote.

40

Spend Student Loans only on School Expenses

It is inherent in its name: a student loan should be used for student expenses only. Although it may be tempting to use student loan money for college football tickets, midnight pizza while cramming for finals, or a Florida spring-break trip, try to resist this lure. You may argue that relaxation, concentration, and performance are ultimately enhanced by these expenditures, so they should be considered school-related expenses. But this argument has a sobering reality. By using student loans for expenses other than direct school-related items, you are only succeeding in getting yourself more deeply in debt. Since the cost of college can be daunting enough, why would you want to add more debt to the amount you will already be required to pay back after graduation?

When Faith was in the process of filling out her student-loan applications, she knew that she had no choice but to rely heavily on this form of monetary assistance in order to be able to afford college. Unfortunately, her parents made too much money for Faith to qualify for any grants. Equally unfortunate was the sad fact that they had consistently spent every dime they made and consequently had not saved up anything for Faith's college education.

Faith wasn't sure how much her tuition, room and board, books, lab fees, and other school-related expenses would be, but she decided to play it safe and borrow the maximum amount available to her. It turned out that this sum was quite substantial. In fact, the check was the largest she had ever received in her life.

Her immediate obligations were to pay for tuition and her dorm's room and board. Then she needed to purchase books and pay for other class materials. With the basic school expenses covered, Faith realized that her checking account was still pretty flush with money from her loan. Surely she could afford to spend a small percentage of her student-loan money on some "extras" to make her demanding and stressful life a little more enjoyable.

With this philosophy in mind, Faith decided to buy a health-club membership. Even though the university's gym was free, she preferred the aerobics classes that were given at a nearby private health club. Also, after only a few weeks of living in her dorm, Faith determined that it was too noisy to study there effectively. Even though the library was a great alternative location to study in and only a short walk from her dorm, she chose to move to an off-campus apartment instead.

Once in her furnished apartment, she bought a *feng shui* book and came to the conclusion that her furniture and its placement were creating negative energy. Unless she bought and rearranged the appropriate furnishings, she would not be able to perform up to her full potential. Her grades would suffer. This revelation resulted in numerous trips to furniture and appliance stores.

In time, Faith's little "extras" cost her quite a substantial sum of money. In fact, she ran out of money halfway through the semester. Her next installment from her student loan was not scheduled to come until January and it was only October. Faith was incredulous that she had gone through her student loan so quickly; after all, it had been such a large check.

Faith literally ran to the financial aid office to request another student loan to help her in the interim. When they told her that she had already received the maximum amount allowed per semester she panicked. "How am I supposed to survive?" she lamented. A financial counselor sat down with Faith, and together they put together a budget of Faith's living expenses. The solution was not one that fit into Faith's philosophy of "adding the little extras."

The extras had to go. Faith had to find a roommate to split her rent, cancel her gym membership, and stop buying furniture and other nonessential personal items. And if she worked part-time at night, she would just make it to January without starving. So much for her hopes of reducing the stresses of her demanding student life. Her freewheeling spending habits had actually increased her stress, not reduced it.

Like Faith, many students apply for the maximum amount of student-loan money available to them. Upon receiving such a large check, they are often tempted by the funds that they now have free access to. Even though they understand these funds are for school-related expenses, life's many spending opportunities get in the way of their clear judgment.

Before accepting a student loan, it is imperative that all school-related expenses be calculated. These may include tuition, textbooks, and room and board. When this amount is known, any financial assistance already committed should be subtracted. This assistance could be in the form of scholarships, part-time campus jobs, summer job income, or money from parents.

If there is still a shortage after the assistance is factored in, you may still need to get additional student loans. However, the amount requested should be only enough to erase the difference. If you receive a larger loan then you need, the temptation to spend the extra money on "fun" things can be hard or even impossible to resist.

41

Develop a Credit History During College

This advice may seem unwise. You've probably heard some horrifying statistics and stories about college students and credit-card debt. In 2000, 78 percent of undergraduate students had credit cards and the average debt on them was $2,748, according to Nellie Mae, a student loan agency. In addition, one out of ten undergraduates owed more than $7,000.

The stories are equally worrisome. Tales abound of parents bailing out their kids from credit-card debt amassed during college. There are also innumerable accounts of students having to cut back to part-time status or drop out of school altogether to make enough money to pay off their balances. Then there are the much-publicized stories about students committing suicide over their credit-card debt. In some cases, these students owed only several thousand dollars.

Therefore, you may have decided that it is not worth the risk to get a credit card during college. You are going to wait until you have graduated, are more mature, and have a full-time job before you get your first credit card. Although this may seem like a wise decision, it may hurt you in the short run.

Jerry's parents grilled him about the dangers of credit cards. They had reason to worry, because Jerry's older sister Paula abused credit cards while she was in school. Her parents ended up bailing Paula out of credit-card debt when they discovered that she owed $5,000 after only her freshman year. They were determined not to repeat this scenario with Jerry.

Jerry listened to his parents' lectures and managed to resist all the credit card offers he routinely saw on campus. Although it was hard on the occasions when his friends would just whip out their credit cards to pay for clothes or drinks at the bar, Jerry knew he had made the right decision when he started to see many of them get into serious debt. Too many of his friends ended up in the same situation his sister Paula had found herself in.

Once Jerry had graduated, he started working full-time and promptly opened a checking and savings account. At the same time he applied for his new bank's credit card; he was declined. The reason for being declined was his lack of a revolving credit history. Other than his student loans, Jerry's credit report was clean.

In disbelief, Jerry decided to try and obtain other credit offers. He picked up credit card applications wherever he saw them—at the dry cleaners, his gym, at restaurants. He filled out the applications and waited. Unbelievably, he was rejected for every credit card that he applied for.

Jerry couldn't understand what he had done wrong. In fact, he thought he had done everything right. He had no credit problems, hadn't gotten into trouble with spending money, and had a respectable job. In spite of all this, he was being penalized for his lack of credit. It was a catch-22 situation. In the world of credit, if you have no credit history you can't get a credit card. But you need a credit card in order to build a credit history. Jerry had encountered the same problem in trying to get his first job.

To add insult to injury, Jerry found himself having to pay deposits to his cell phone company ($400) and to his utility company ($100) because he was a first-time user with no credit history. It was turning out to be quite costly not having a credit card before graduation.

Adding to the monetary costs were the costs to his bruised ego. He was bound and determined to be independent of his parents, only to find that he needed their help. Jerry eventually gave in and asked his parents to co-sign on a credit card for him. For Jerry this was more humiliating than being rejected by the credit card companies.

Since not having a credit history makes post-college life more complicated and more expensive, it is worth obtaining a credit card during your college years. It is usually easy to get one while you are a college student, regardless of whether you have a job or reliable source of income.

Once you get one, however, it is important to remember the rules of wise credit card usage (Chapter 33). There is a middle ground in which students can build a credit history in college, have the convenience of using credit instead of cash for purchases and emergencies, and still not run up a lot of debt. The bottom line is that you can work out a win-win situation when it comes to credit cards.

Till Debt
Do Us Part

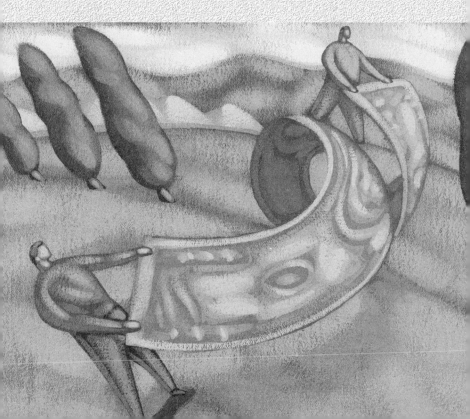

42

Share Your Financial Situation with Your Roommate

Regardless of whether your roommate is sharing expenses with you or being supported by you, he or she needs to know if you are having financial problems. Your ability to pay household bills and contribute to other financial obligations directly impacts the people you live with. For example, if you are not able to live up to your part of the bargain, someone else must cover the shortfall. Your roommate's budget may be overwhelmed if he or she is suddenly asked to pay the entire rent instead of just half.

In most cases, the main reason for choosing to live with a roommate is a financial one. Although some people prefer the company, most consider it an inconvenience to give up their privacy. They do it, however, in order to share the financial burden and be able to live in a place that they couldn't afford on their own.

I found myself in the financial predicament of needing a roommate shortly after moving to Los Angeles. I chose to move there after graduate school because I had grown up in the Midwest and desperately wanted to escape the cold. I decided to share an apartment with a friend of mine from college who had escaped to Los Angeles for the very same reason. We were close friends in college, and I thought I knew Kristen very well. However, I soon learned that she harbored a secret that she had successfully hidden from me for many years.

That secret was the fact that she had an eating disorder—bulimia. This disorder caused her to eat large quantities of food as she engaged in the cycle of binging and purging. Besides the many serious psychological and health issues associated with this disorder, it caused grave financial issues as well.

The less serious issue was the fact that we split the cost of groceries but I rarely got a chance to eat the food because Kristen consumed it so quickly. It was very annoying to come home from work hungry and open an empty refrigerator. The more serious issue, however, was that her restaurant tabs in addition to her grocery spending used up a large portion of her paycheck. Before I knew it, Kristen was not able to pay her half of the rent. This created an emergency because my first job out of college was a low-paying, entry-level one and I couldn't afford to pay the entire rent on my minuscule salary.

I somehow was able to cover her half of the rent for one month, but when the next month arrived and Kristen still didn't have her half of the rent, I knew I was in trouble. Not knowing what else to do I called Kristen's parents, whom I had met many times during college. They agreed to send Kristen the rent money. Their check arrived, but the money was literally eaten up as it was used for food and not rent. This is when I decided to move out. Unfortunately, the landlord wouldn't give me back my security deposit since it was held to cover our rent shortage.

My friendship with Kristen was destroyed. I was angry that she hadn't shared with me her eating disorder, which was the root cause of her money troubles. If I had known, I could have tried to get her to seek professional counseling, or at the very least I would have received a warning about her tendency to spend most of her money on food. This pattern was not new; it had continued since her first paying job in high school. However, Kristen chose to remain silent until the situation inevitably became visible and she could hide it no longer.

Many believe that keeping their roommate or loved one in the dark about their financial predicament protects these people from worry. This strategy tends to be counterproductive, since if people believe everything is all right they will continue with their normal money behavior. If the way out of a financial crisis involves a reduction in spending, this cannot be accomplished by one person alone—everyone must work together as a team. Shielding roommates and loved ones from a financial crisis only delays the inevitable day when the truth will come out. The delay may result in the situation becoming aggravated.

So swallow your pride and remember that it is a rare individual who never has financial problems. Your roommates or loved ones may actually have great advice if they had to work their way out of a similar predicament. When it comes to shared finances, honesty is crucial not only for your financial well-being but also for the well-being of the relationship.

43

Divorce Should Never Be About Money

The number-one reason for divorce in this country is "fighting about money." As Chapter 34 demonstrated, Anna and Martin's first real fight in their marriage was over money. It is understandable that financial difficulties can cause incredible strain in a relationship, but in many cases the situation is temporary and can be resolved if the couple works together as a team. Unfortunately, the opposite often occurs as the couple points fingers and assigns blame for the current state of affairs.

The finger-pointing was getting ugly during a credit counseling session for Ken and Joan. Neither could accept any responsibility for their debt crisis, and their continual shifting of the blame was counterproductive as it distracted the discussion from finding a solution. In Ken's mind their problems were entirely the fault of his wife, since she had charged up the vast majority of their credit-card debt. However, their level of credit-card debt was equaled by the two home-equity lines of credit that Ken had taken out.

Ken countered that he was forced to get home-equity loans to pay off his wife's credit-card debt. In response, Joan protested that she never knew this and besides, Ken in no way told her to curtail her spending. She, in fact, thought their finances were in fantastic shape. Since Ken took care of all the household financial responsibilities, including paying the bills and budgeting, Joan was ignorant of their financial problems until the collection agencies started calling the house.

The credit counselor tried to get them to stop the blame game by pointing out that both of them were at some fault in their predicament. It was true that Joan's spending contributed to their debt problems, but Ken should have been honest with her about his financial capacity. If Ken had shared the family budget with Joan, she would have realized her spending limitations. Instead, Ken chose to remain quiet and pay off her initial debts by acquiring more debt.

The one thing that is certain in life is that following the same path will lead to the same destination. In order for Ken to have changed the outcome after he used home-equity loans as a short-term solution, he would have had to either get a huge raise at his job or curtail his wife's spending severely. Unfortunately, he chose neither of these directions and the same path led them down the debt road again, which eventually led to the credit counselor's office.

Ironically, working together to improve the family's money troubles can actually strengthen a partnership. Regardless of the reason for the financial situation (the problem could have been caused directly by one partner's overspending or indirectly by one partner being laid off from work), once the cause is identified a solution can be agreed upon. By jointly focusing on the problem, partners can provide support to each other. One partner might need a reminder to resist the temptation to buy something; the other partner might need encouragement as he or she works overtime to get extra money.

If both partners are truly committed to the cause, there is nothing like a good struggle to ensure bonding. The payoff comes at the end, when the financial crisis has been solved and when both partners can equally rejoice in their success since they did it together. Money problems can be overcome and resolved much more easily than other marital issues like incompatibility or spousal abuse. Those issues may eventually lead to divorce, but money issues should never be the primary motivation for divorce. You promised as much when you repeated "for richer or for poorer."

44

Check Your future Spouse's Credit Report

It may be a good idea to request your spouse-to-be's credit report prior to saying "I do." You can't legally request another person's report (unless he or she is applying for credit with you), but it would be a good idea to ask your partner to request it. Far too many newlyweds are shocked to discover that their new spouse has excessive debt, child-support and alimony obligations, or has even filed bankruptcy. Millie, a twenty-five-year-old New Yorker, learned this news the hard way.

Millie knew that Ted had children from a previous marriage. She had never met them, though, because they lived in another state. In fact, in the two years that Millie had known Ted before they got married, he had only visited them twice. Millie had asked to go along on the second trip, but Ted insisted that his ex-wife was hostile and he wanted to spare Millie from witnessing her behavior. When Millie pressed to find out why his ex-wife was so hostile, Ted cryptically responded that she had "issues." Millie figured it was a painful topic, so she just dropped it.

Shortly after his marriage to Millie, Ted got into a car accident when another driver abruptly pulled out in front of him. Ted was not injured, but his car was totaled. Needing another car to replace his totaled one, Ted got a ride from Millie to the car dealer. Ted finally chose a car that he wanted, but when it came time to work out the financing he asked Millie to wait outside the office. She didn't want to be excluded from something so important to the couple's finances, so she insisted on being *inside* the office while the negotiations were conducted.

Millie soon discovered why Ted didn't want her in the office. When it came time to review Ted's credit report, it was revealed that he had been delinquent in his child-support payments. He was so delinquent that his ex-wife was forced to file an order with the district attorney's office. This resulted in Ted's wages being garnished by 20 percent. Millie knew what Ted's salary was, but she had no idea that he was actually taking home 20 percent less than she thought he was. To make matters worse, Ted had to accept a very high interest rate of 36 percent on his car loan because his credit was so bad.

Now not only was Ted's ex-wife hostile, but his current one was also. By hiding this information from Millie and not being honest prior to their marriage, Ted only succeeded in delaying the inevitable. If you are married, chances are that your spouse will discover your credit history sooner or later. Believe me, sooner is better than later!

We learned in Chapter 34 (it can't be restated enough) that even though the legal responsibility for debt acquired prior to a marriage cannot transfer to the new spouse, both will face the reality of the indebtedness. One spouse may have to help the other pay off the debt because the debt load is a drag on the couple's financial situation. The couple will need to work as a team to pay off this debt since their ability to save depends on it.

In Millie's case, she needed to learn how to cope with a 20 percent reduction in Ted's salary. She needed to start adjusting her spending downward, since in reality they now had less money to work with. Knowing the facts prior to taking the plunge is not only prudent but will start the marriage off with honesty—which you may find to be priceless.

45

Don't Start Your Married Life with Excessive Wedding Debt

Many people want their wedding to be perfect . . . regardless of the cost. They hire the most expensive band and the best caterer in town, reserve the most elegant reception hall, buy a designer wedding dress, and book a honeymoon at a five-star resort. When you add up all the costs that go into a formal wedding, they can be significant. If you cringed at the cost of the wedding ring, remember that that expense is minuscule in comparison to an elaborate wedding.

It is not uncommon for even a simple wedding to cost at least $10,000 and for an over-the-top wedding to cost $100,000 or more. In the first case, that money could have purchased a car and in the latter case, that money could have gone toward the purchase of a home. Whereas a wedding lasts only a day, a car or home will be with you for much longer. Some people may argue that the memory of a wedding is something that stays with you forever. This may be true, but in terms of a tangible asset a memory is not something that will bring you to work in the morning or put a roof over your head at night.

Lisa and Joe viewed their wedding as a once-in-a-lifetime, no-holds-barred, blowout event. They didn't concern themselves with cost. They just made their selections and asked that everything be billed to them or put on their credit cards. It was hard to keep track of how much they were spending, however, since the preparations were getting quite complicated. They made a decision to not worry about it until after the wedding. Besides, they didn't want anything to put a damper on their excitement.

The day of their wedding finally arrived, and the guests were not disappointed. Every detail was attended to, from the doves that were released into the sky to the expensive party favors that were handed out. Each corner of the large banquet hall had a delicacy to choose from. One corner had shrimp and caviar, another had lobster tails, and yet another had filet mignon. The highlight of the evening was a fifteen-minute film of the bride and groom's lives from their birth to the present. Old home movies had been edited together along with music and a script. It was quite a production.

The guests wondered how such a young couple could afford such a wedding, since Lisa and Joe had been out of college for only a few years. Their first jobs were typical for recent college graduates—entry-level jobs with correspondingly low salaries. The guests just assumed that their parents had been very generous.

Although their parents had helped out with some of the expenses, they had drawn the line on paying for what they considered the "extravagances" that their children saw as necessities. They tried to encourage their children to simplify their wedding, but Lisa and Joe were insistent. They wanted what they wanted, and if their parents wouldn't help out they would just have to find a way to pay for it themselves.

Their solution of using credit to finance their wedding succeeded in making possible the wedding they desired, but it also succeeded in putting them seriously in debt. Afterwards, they could no longer procrastinate in dealing with their wedding finances so they sat down and counted up the cost of their wedding. The bottom line was shocking. They knew that their wedding was on the expensive side; they just had no idea how expensive. The total cost to Lisa and Joe (excluding what their parents paid for) was around $40,000.

They panicked because they knew it was impossible on their limited incomes to pay back this huge amount right away. They decided that Joe should make phone calls to arrange payment plans in order to pay off their debts over time. Some creditors refused and insisted on immediate payment. Those creditors were paid with Lisa and Joe's credit cards. This only succeeded in moving debt from one place to another.

In the end they were able to negotiate payment plans that they could handle. Unfortunately, this debt load prevented Lisa and Joe from adding any other debts to it. This meant that their aging cars would have to last for a lot longer and their dream of buying their own place instead of renting would also have to wait. They had wanted to start a family right away, but the cost of having children would have put them over the edge. With so many of their dreams on hold, they couldn't help but wonder in retrospect if they had made the right decision to have such an elaborate wedding.

How you choose to spend your hard-earned money is an individual choice, and a fancy wedding may be a high priority for you. Just keep in mind that the money you and your spouse-to-be spend at the start of your life together is money that will then not be available for your immediate or future goals. If your parents foot the bill for the wedding, they might not be able to help you out financially with other goals like a down payment for your first house.

The emotions that go along with a wedding are powerful, and sometimes motivations like jealousy, inadequacy, or even envy can interfere with rational spending behavior. Do an honest assessment of the reasons why you "need" to have such an expensive wedding. You may discover that you are trying to compete with your cousin's wedding or that you want to project an image of success and wealth to your guests. Regardless of the motivation behind the excessive spending, the consequences are the same—a life together starting off deeply in debt. With a substantial debt burden to contend with, other goals like buying a house and having children may have to wait.

46

Don't Have Children Before You Can Afford Them

With the cost of raising and putting a child through college at upwards of one million dollars, the decision to start a family should not be based solely on emotions. A rational appraisal of your household's financial capacity to handle the additional expenses should also be conducted. You should know the costs involved before the baby is even conceived, not after.

Eileen and Jim had always agreed that they wanted a big family. Jim came from a large family that was very close, and Eileen, an only child, envied their relationships. They decided to start having children immediately after their marriage. Eileen was already twenty-four years old, and with the six children they planned on having, the clock was ticking. They had to start now before Eileen's age limited the number of children she was able to conceive.

They were lucky and Eileen got pregnant almost immediately. She was working full-time but quit her job after the baby was born. This effectively cut their income in half, but they were confident they could manage on Jim's salary alone. It helped that their initial baby expenses were minimal since Jim's brothers and sisters, who already had children, gave them many donations and hand-me-downs.

As their lives started to settle into a pattern, they began to realize that the actual costs of having a baby were more than they had anticipated. They never dreamed that diapers and formula could add up to so much. Without Eileen's income to help, Jim felt an enormous strain being the sole supporter of the family. Nevertheless, they did not deviate from their initial plan and Eileen became pregnant again.

Now their costs were double. Jim found that his income was not enough to cover the expenses. He had to find another part-time job on top of his full-time job. He was working so much that he was rarely home. Eileen found herself the full-time caregiver for the babies without any break. Whenever Jim came home, he was exhausted and wanted only to rest. But Eileen saw his arrival as a chance for her to get some much-needed rest also. Obviously someone had to watch the children, and it became a daily argument over who it would be.

The financial stress contributed to their marital stress, and it almost broke their marriage apart. They then made a decision to limit their family to two children for the moment. Their goal of six would have been impossible given their financial limitations—and their emotional limits as well. In addition, they started to ask for baby-sitting help from Jim's large family.

Many new parents are shocked when they discover all the purchases they must make prior to their baby being born. They need at a minimum a crib, clothes, diaper bag, shoes, baby bottles, and a car seat. This list doesn't even include all the additional "necessities" that families usually purchase like a baby swing, toys, cute little hats, and a myriad of other baby stuff. If you've ever chosen a gift from a baby-register list, you have probably been astonished by the quantity of items to choose from. These initial purchases can be overwhelming to new parents.

Baby showers can be a wonderful way to help reduce the parents' initial costs, but what about their ongoing expenses? After the baby shower is over, who will pay for the formula, the diapers, the larger clothes, and the baby-sitters? And this is just the start. Another important consideration is the cost of child care if both parents continue to work. As the children grow, so do their expenses. Soon you will be worrying about how to pay for their first car or their college education.

Don't assume the money drain will end after college. What about their wedding or their requests for money to help them pay off their credit-card debt? Although your living expenses will improve when your child moves out (lower grocery costs, phone bill), you may find that other child-related expenses just take their place.

It is important to realize that not only will the family's budget have the added expenditures related to child-rearing to contend with, but the income side of the budget may also be affected. If one parent decides to stay home full-time instead of working, the family's total available income will be reduced. Without contemplating the new budget reality that having a child will impose, the resulting financial stress could be significant.

47

Always Discuss Major Purchases with Your Spouse

If your husband has unilaterally decided to use your income-tax refund to buy a new motorcycle without discussing it with you first, the surprise upon seeing a motorcycle in the driveway may not be a pleasant one. You may have had other ideas of how you wanted to spend or invest that same tax-refund check. Maybe you wanted to use the refund to pay down credit-card debt or go on a Caribbean vacation. When major purchases are being considered, it is always wise to discuss the options as a couple.

Dana got such a surprise when she arrived home one evening. It wasn't a motorcycle in the driveway, however, but a brand-new BMW. At first she thought her husband, Eric, had a friend over, but the car was not familiar. Maybe one of his friends had just bought a new car and come over to show it off. "They must be doing well to be able to afford such a car," she thought to herself.

When she entered the house she found her husband watching TV all by himself. "Who's over?" she asked. "No one," he responded. It immediately hit her when Eric produced a huge smile that the car was his. Dana started to feel a knot in her stomach because she was the one who handled the couple's finances. "How much are the monthly payments?" she nervously inquired. "Oh, only about $500 a month," Eric replied without hesitation.

Dana's fears were confirmed. She didn't know how they were going to be able to make the payments. Their current budget left an extra cushion of only $300 a month after all the bills were paid. Now they were going to be $200 short each month and have no extra money to pay for anything "fun" like dinners out or entertainment. They would be virtual slaves to this car payment for the next five years (the length of Eric's lease).

Dana had no choice but to live with Eric's purchase since they couldn't return the car. She inquired, but the lease he signed didn't have a three-day cancellation policy. They were stuck with it. In order to make the car payment, Dana had to cut out other expenses in their budget. She cancelled their cable TV, newspaper subscription, health club membership, golf lessons, and many other expenses considered "nonessential." They lost many of the pleasures that they had enjoyed before. Whenever Dana saw the new car in the driveway, it was a reminder of what they had given up.

Dana's resentment over Eric's car usually erupted around the time of the month when she paid their bills. One month Eric couldn't take the guilt anymore and made the decision to get rid of the car any way that he could. Eric found a solution through a friend who he knew was looking for a new car. His friend took over Eric's lease and continued to make the payments, thereby freeing up Eric from his responsibility.

When Dana came home one day, she found another surprise in the driveway. This time, however, it was a pleasant surprise. Eric had purchased a used car with payments that were only $200 a month. This freed up the $300 that had been committed to his BMW, and it allowed them to add back into their lives some of the pleasures they had given up. With the financial stress eliminated from their marriage, they found their relationship improved. Eric vowed to involve his wife in all future major purchases.

Even if you tend to handle all the monetary transactions yourself, the decisions regarding goals should always be handled as a couple. The first step is to find out what one another's goals are. Very rarely do couples sit down and ask this important question. But each of us tends to be highly motivated by visions of what we desire. We might be dreaming of that Caribbean vacation while we work overtime. The overtime is welcomed since it becomes a means to an end. If your spouse does not realize that your dream of a Caribbean vacation is being made possible through your hours of overtime, he or she might resent the time spent apart.

After you ask the "goal" question you might discover that one partner wants children, overseas vacations, and a house, while the other partner wants a substantial retirement fund, tailored suits, or an advanced degree. When inconsistencies arrive, a compromise may be necessary. If you have different but compatible goals, you can then work out a plan to reach both partners' goals. This will require prioritizing the goals so that if money limits the number of reachable goals, at least they will be the most important ones.

If you have incompatible goals, you may need to compromise or make a decision where only one partner ends up being happy. An example is the goal of one partner obtaining an advanced degree but the other wanting to pay off debt and not incur more. It may turn out that the compromise is an advanced degree achieved through night classes that allows the partner to continue working. Or the goals of the nonstudent partner may have to be put on hold for a while until the advanced degree is completed. Then the degree may result in a promotion, and the extra money will go toward the other partner's goals for a while; his or her patience will then be rewarded.

The important lesson to learn is that decisions regarding major purchases must be made together. Identification of goals, plans to reach them, and the money to pay for them are mutual decisions, not individual ones. Otherwise, the anger or hurt feelings generated from decisions made without consulting the other may greatly damage the relationship.

48

Don't Hide Purchases from Your Significant Other

Is it better to conceal a purchase from your partner if you know he or she will not approve of the buy? For instance, many women prefer to mingle new clothes among the old in the closet or hide them under the bed. Concealing purchases is generally easier for women than it is for men because women tend to shop more often but buy smaller things.

On the other hand, men spend less often but buy bigger and more expensive items. While a woman may hide a new dress quite easily, a man has a much harder time hiding his new motorcycle! Evasion can be a way to avoid immediate confrontation, but this stalling technique can backfire when the purchases are eventually discovered.

Jenna was an expert at evasion because her husband, Oscar, had a fit every time she spent money. Oscar was a passionate investor in the stock market, and he religiously invested all of their extra money each month. But in fact he only "thought" he invested all of their extra money. In reality, Jenna had a side income that he knew nothing about.

Just after they had married, Oscar explained that consistent investing was the only way to assure they would have a prosperous retirement. Jenna had a hard time focusing on retirement—after all, they were only twenty-two years old. However, she was proud of the fact that her husband was so diligent and worried about their future. After a year of marriage however, Jenna started to resent his rigid spending limitations and she longed to spend money frivolously.

Because she had to turn her paycheck over to Oscar, since he did all the bookkeeping, Jenna decided to amass a secret slush fund. She was a writer and started to take some editing projects on the side. She would just stay late at the office to do her editing jobs and explain to Oscar that her job was requiring longer and longer hours.

This slush fund was money that she used only on herself. She would buy new clothes, makeup, and shoes at the mall. Jenna loved to shop, and since Oscar had deprived her of this pleasure for an entire year, she felt she needed to make up for lost time. She shopped as religiously as he invested.

At first the purchases were easy to hide in the closet since it was just an outfit or two, but in time the closet started becoming more and more crowded and it was becoming noticeable. Oscar was not very observant, however, and when he asked if an outfit was new Jenna would just reply, "Oh, this old thing? I just haven't worn it in awhile."

After one shopping spree Jenna was careless and didn't take the price tag off one of the dresses. Oscar noticed, and it triggered his suspicions. He started to go through their closets and bathroom demanding to know if each item was a new purchase. Eventually Jenna confessed.

After the deceit was out in the open, Oscar wanted to know how she funded these purchases. She then had to explain her side job, which made Oscar even more angry. Jenna's explanation about feeling constrained by Oscar's frugal spending fell on deaf ears since he now felt betrayed. Now Jenna found herself having to confront an even bigger problem than Oscar's frugality—his lack of trust.

If your spouse is observant, he or she may remark on your new outfit or notice a new purchase when it appears on the credit card statement. Any anger that may have resulted from your spending the money in the first place will be exacerbated by the attempt at deceit. A frank conversation about why you felt compelled to conceal the purchase·in the first place is the best way to bring the issue out in the open and out of the closet.

49

Get Married and Stay Married

A divorce rarely improves your financial situation; it usually results in making it worse. The main reason is that one household to support has been split into two. Instead of one residence, the separated parties must now live apart. This may involve only one person relocating. On the other hand, if their shared residence is too large for any one party, both may be forced to relocate.

The moving costs may be significant, especially if the breakup involves selling or buying property. Since choosing the right time to buy or sell is not a luxury if a divorce is on the fast track, losses may be inevitable. If the real estate market is especially depressed, the price your house can fetch may be much lower than the price when you bought it. Conversely, the housing market may be so crowded that you can't find a vacancy in the neighborhood you want to live in.

Once resettled, there are now twice as many mortgage or rent payments, electricity bills, and phone bills to pay. It may also be necessary to buy a second car if the household used to share one. This doubling of expenses is made more difficult if only one parent is working. If one parent is a homemaker, this means that the working parent's one income is now responsible for supporting two households.

Karen, age twenty-four, had always paid the bills in the family since she was extremely organized; her husband, Mike, was focused on the big picture. This tendency, she believed, caused him to be careless. One day while paying the credit-card bills, she noticed a charge for a trip to Miami (although Mike had told her that his business trip was to Cincinnati), a flower shop, and a lingerie boutique. This is how she learned her husband was having an affair.

For Karen, there was no such thing as a second chance. She hired a lawyer right away and started the divorce process. Mike, age twenty-five, begged for her to trust him again and not leave him. He assured Karen that he would change and never cheat on her again. Karen reconsidered and ended up deciding to stay with Mike, but for reasons that were solely financial.

As she was going through the figures with her lawyer, she came to the horrifying conclusion that they were too poor to divorce. Mike was the sole wage earner (Karen stayed home with the children), and on his income alone he could adequately support the household. But if Mike were required to support two households on his income, Karen discovered she wouldn't receive enough child support from him to make ends meet. Not wanting her two children, ages two and four, to suffer a significant decrease in their standard of living, Karen decided to stay with Mike.

Further supporting the decision was her concern that since she had no credit in her name, she might have trouble establishing credit. Since all their credit cards were in Mike's name, she lacked a credit history. It is always wise to obtain credit in your own name so that you can become financially independent and not rely on your spouse's credit history. This is particularly true if the spouse has a blemished credit history. It may be a detriment and may not accurately reflect your timely payment habits.

As the years went on, Karen learned of other affairs her husband was having. His promise to her to never stray again had turned out to be false. Without seeking professional help, he could not change his compulsion to cheat. Karen felt financially trapped, forced to live in the same house with a man she distrusted and had begun to despise.

It is a rare case when a divorce results in a financial bonanza for one of the parties. Situations where this can occur tend to be in wealthy households where the breadwinner is required to pay large alimony or child-support payments. This situation is the exception, however, and not the rule. In fact, according to the National Center for Women and Retirement, women experience a 45 percent average decline in their lifestyle the year following a divorce.

Obviously, if a marriage is extremely unhappy, a divorce is the right thing to do for emotional reasons alone. Staying in an unloving marriage is harmful for all parties involved, including the children. But the reality is that although the emotional situation may improve after a divorce, the financial situation may not.

50

You Can't Buy Love

You've probably heard this expression before. Maybe you heard it from your mom, or maybe it was your minister. Regardless of who told you "You can't buy love," chances are that you didn't really believe it. The problem is that there is abundant evidence to the contrary.

Most gossip and celebrity magazines carry pictures of the rich and famous with their beautiful and usually much younger spouses at their side. Seeing them, you probably leap to the conclusion that these are marriages not for love but for money. To further substantiate your belief, when these marriages fall apart you say, "See, he (or she) was just after the money."

Although there is no way to determine how many people actually marry for money and not love (most people wouldn't admit it even if it was true), there are enough cases to cause you to disagree with your mother or minister and say, "Yes, you can buy love."

Barry believed that money would make anything and everything possible. He was convinced that with money he would be able to overcome many of his outward flaws. Even though he was valedictorian of his high school and went on to graduate with honors at Purdue University, he was thought of as short and pudgy first and smart a distant second.

It made him angry that his hard work and intelligence were not appreciated more. All his life it seemed that the guys with the looks got everything they wanted without even trying. They were the ones with the popular girls on their arms. They were the ones in college who were picked to join the best fraternity houses. "It's not fair," Barry had lamented.

Since Barry was convinced he could never compete with these guys on looks and personality alone, he decided to concentrate on his best asset—his intelligence. This decision led to law school and then to a position at a large law firm in Chicago. Barry rapidly advanced in the firm as he took on larger and larger caseloads. His efforts were rewarded several years later when he was made partner.

Along with his partner status came a large salary increase. This enabled Barry to buy a luxury condominium with a view of Lake Michigan. His salary also enabled him to join an exclusive social club, where he met other people of similar means. It was through these connections that he met Betsy.

Betsy was not a member of the social club, but she was a friend of Rick and Cheryl, members of the club who had befriended Barry. The couple organized a dinner party so that Barry could meet Betsy. When he first saw her, he was stunned by her beauty. His immediate thought was that she would never be interested in him. When she turned out to be not only interested but also seemingly hanging on his every word, Barry couldn't believe his good fortune.

They started dating, and in no time Betsy had moved herself into Barry's condominium. Even though they were living together, Barry still had fears of Betsy changing her mind at any time and leaving him. In order to make sure she stayed, Barry asked Betsy to marry him. She promptly said yes.

When Barry called Rick to tell him the good news, Barry was shocked by his response. Instead of being supportive of the engagement, Barry's friend tried to talk him out of it. Rick said that Betsy was a "gold-digger." It turned out that Betsy had confided to Cheryl that she didn't really love Barry but she desperately wanted the lifestyle that he could afford. Cheryl, even though sworn to secrecy, had in turn told Rick.

At first Barry was crushed by this news, but then he convinced himself that in time Betsy would certainly grow to love him. As the years went by, Betsy's feelings toward Barry did change. Unfortunately, they changed for the worse and not the better. She grew to dislike him more and more.

Barry responded by trying to please her the only way he knew how—buying possessions. He bought her a new Mercedes, expensive jewelry, and designer furnishings for their home. He even bought a larger condo with a better view of the lake in order to make Betsy happy.

Despite all these efforts to buy her love, it didn't work. Betsy eventually filed for divorce and fought mightily for a large monetary settlement. In the end, after their divorce was final, Betsy ended up with exactly what she wanted in the first place—Barry's money.

The moral of the story is that the saying "You can't buy love" is both true and false. You may succeed in initially buying love with money. As long as there continue to be people who are looking to marry into wealth, this possibility exists. But in the long run, the only thing that will keep a marriage sustainable is love. Without love, the fish that you succeed in catching may long to be cast back into the sea.

The Rainy Day: Finding Your Umbrella

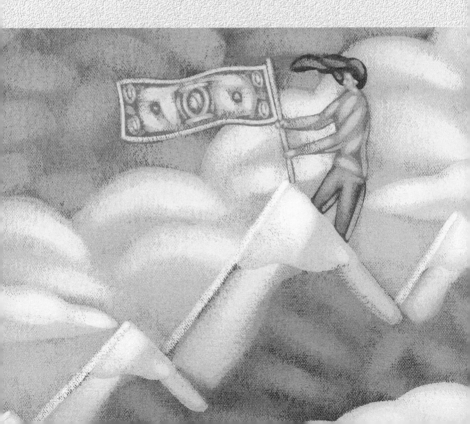

51

Have an Emergency Fund

Life events can and do happen; you can count on it. These blips in the road of life are sometimes small potholes and other times large chasms. The potholes can be annoyances that divert you briefly from your path. But the chasms can result in your having to backtrack, delaying the arrival at your intended destination. Life events are the blips in your financial roadmap. These unexpected occurrences result in expenditures you were not planning on and can wreak havoc on your budget.

If you think that life events don't happen to you, engage in some honest reflection on the events over the past year. Did you get a speeding or parking ticket? What about car repairs? Did that Internet start-up that was supposed to make you millions end up sending you to the unemployment line instead? Did your pet get sick or hurt and have to be taken to the vet? I sometimes think that veterinarians are so expensive because they know their clients would never deny their pets care. I know many people who avoid the doctor when they themselves get sick but would never consider passing up medical care for their pets.

All of life's "life events" never seem to happen when you are prepared. They always seem to occur when you are the most vulnerable. For example, if you got downsized from an industry that has tanked and you have no other skills, it might be necessary to go back to school to acquire new marketable skills. Now not only have you lost an income, you have added expenses from college tuition to compound your problem. It is smarter to act under the premise that life events are inevitable rather than thinking you are a lucky person and bad things will pass you by. I've never met anyone who's had that much luck!

Brenda did not plan for the future. Whether it would turn out to be good or bad did not concern her; she just lived in the moment. Living in and appreciating the present is actually an admirable trait. So few of us do it. We are usually regretting the past or worrying about the future. But it is possible to live in the present and plan for the future at the same time. One is not mutually exclusive of the other. Brenda, on the other hand, only concerned herself with the here and now.

Brenda's present revolved around her boyfriend, Lee. They lived together in an apartment in Manhattan Beach, California. Brenda was much younger than Lee and was still in college. Since Lee was already out in the working world, he paid for their combined living expenses. Brenda did not take college seriously because she didn't plan on having a career. She was totally content with her current situation and assumed she would eventually become Lee's wife and he would continue to take care of her.

Unfortunately, Brenda's perfect world crumbled after Lee decided he wanted his independence. This decision affected Brenda in two ways. Not only did she lose her boyfriend, but she lost her boyfriend's income as well. Having just graduated from college she needed to find a job, but Brenda had no idea what she wanted to do. She had never given her career path any serious consideration. Brenda ended up working at a coffee shop out of necessity. This might not have happened if she had approached her future reality with a strategy.

Without a financial safety net in place, the options out of a monetary predicament are limited. You might be forced to get an immediate job (any job) like Brenda, just to pay the bills. If you don't have any accessible savings, you have several other equally undesirable options you could resort to.

The first option would be to pull money out of your inaccessible savings account. This account is inaccessible because it contains money earmarked solely for your retirement years. You can draw money out early, but the penalties are substantial. The other undesirable option is to use credit to finance the life event. For instance, if you don't have the cash to pay for new tires for your car, you may pay for them with your credit card. If you only make the minimum payment when you receive the bill, these tires may turn out to be extremely expensive by the time you add in the cost of interest. You could have easily bought tires for *two* cars for the same eventual cost if you had paid cash instead of using credit.

Therefore, the most desirable option is to have a savings cushion in place that is equal to three to six months of your monthly expenditures. For instance, if your expenses are $2,000 a month, you should have $6,000 to $12,000 in an accessible account (one without penalties for early withdrawal). With a financial safety net in place, "life events" will not make you so desperate. The knowledge that you have money available to give you a temporary reprieve from the bill collectors is a comforting one that will give you peace of mind.

52

Never Hide from the Bill Collector

The old adage "What we don't see can't hurt us" is a fallacy, especially when it comes to money. Avoiding creditors or not coming to terms with the reality of your situation only serves to make matters worse. A more accurate adage is "You can run but you can't hide." This is because the bill collector will eventually find you.

Your capture is a foregone conclusion because the creditors have many legal tactics to compel you to pay. Even if you don't end up paying the creditor the amount owed, you will end up paying in other ways. For instance, if the creditor has to resort to taking you to court, this will affect your credit report negatively and you will have to pay legal fees. If your car is repossessed, it will most likely be sold in an auction. If the sale price is not enough to cover your existing loan, you will receive a deficiency balance notice in the mail. This difference becomes your responsibility and you will end up paying on a car that you no longer own.

Craig, a twenty-five-year-old fitness trainer, became an expert in this game of hide-and-seek with his creditors. In fact, he relied on his ability to never be found. Craig figured that his creditors would eventually tire of this game and give up. Although this rationale was not logical, Craig convinced himself of its validity. The initial course of events served only to reinforce his way of thinking.

The way that Craig hid was by avoiding any interaction with his creditors. This involved not answering his phone, opening his mail, or responding to legal notices. Craig felt annoyed by this harassment, but he was sure that it couldn't continue forever. Eventually Craig was rewarded for his patience. In time the creditors seemed to have given up, just as he thought they eventually would. Their calls and letters stopped. But Craig forgot that what we don't see *can* hurt us.

One day a moving van appeared at his house. Several men produced a legal order to repossess his fitness equipment. Craig had purchased expensive weight training machines, treadmills, and other fitness necessities in order to train clients at his home. His private clientele base was growing, and he intended to start making payments on the equipment as soon as he was able. But now was not the right time—it was too soon. His creditors had been too impatient; he would eventually pay them.

Unfortunately, his creditors did not have the opportunity to work out alternate payment arrangements with Craig because he never returned their phone calls or responded to their letters. They might have been willing to lower his payments over a longer period of time or allow him to skip a month in order to catch up. However, Craig's lack of response left his creditors no other choice than to repossess the equipment.

This consequence was the worst possible scenario for Craig. He not only lost the ability to make a living since his equipment was now gone, but he also severely ruined his credit report. The negative on his credit report would now appear for seven long years. Craig discovered this fact when he went to purchase additional fitness equipment on credit to replace the things that were repossessed. No other fitness company was willing to give him the equipment on credit because his track record of nonpayment and eventual repossession was not a positive indication of what his future payment pattern would be.

The ostrich syndrome (putting your head in the sand) only makes your problem go away temporarily; it will ultimately return. The best course of action is to always call the creditor *before* the creditor has to call you. Creditors will be more willing to work out payment arrangements if you come to them instead of having to be chased. By running away, you only serve to aggravate the situation by making the creditors angry. You will have succeeded only in neglecting a serious matter and escalating its consequences. It's naive to think that your debts will magically disappear and your creditors will absorb your losses without any consequence to you.

53

Never File for Bankruptcy Without Considering All the options

Bankruptcy should always be the last option, not the first. Unfortunately, many people panic when faced with seemingly insurmountable money problems and think the only way out is through bankruptcy. Ironically this solution, which initially may appear to make your problems disappear, will in fact continue to be a looming presence in your life for many years.

As Vanessa sat in bankruptcy court waiting for her case to be called, it seemed surreal to her that she was there for personal reasons and not professional ones. She was actually a law student and had never envisioned needing the legal services that she now required. "How did it ever get to this point?" was the question she kept asking herself over and over. This was not a difficult question to answer, however, since Vanessa's own decisions were directly responsible for her presence in the courtroom that day.

It all started when Vanessa was a freshman at Illinois State University. She filled out the application for a credit card that was stuffed in her bookstore bag along with her textbook purchases. She rationalized that she needed a credit card for emergencies, so she considered her decision a wise money management move. Unfortunately, it was Vanessa's definition of an emergency that got her into trouble.

Over the next four years, Vanessa experienced an unbelievable number of "emergencies." First there was the spring break trip to Florida, and then there was the personal trainer at the gym. Vanessa charged her dress for a fraternity dance and her drinks at the bar. Before long, almost anything and everything became classified as an emergency.

Vanessa knew that she owed a lot of money, but it didn't concern her as long as she was able to make the minimum payments demanded each month. Besides, she fully intended to pay off the debt after she became a lawyer and started making "big bucks." This plan had one large flaw, however . . . its timeline. Vanessa got into trouble well before she graduated from law school and before she started making "big bucks."

The monthly payment on the debt load that she had accumulated became larger and larger as Vanessa continued to charge her emergencies. Eventually the monthly payment became more than she could manage on her limited student funds. She became further and further behind as she missed payments or sent in less than the required minimum. By this time, Vanessa owed a total of $6,000 on four credit cards. She didn't see how it would be possible to pay back this debt since she was living on minimal student loans and her demanding law school courses didn't leave any extra time to work at a part-time job.

Vanessa was too embarrassed to ask her parents for help. They were very proud of her and constantly bragged to their friends about their smart daughter who was in law school. Vanessa didn't want to disappoint them by revealing that she wasn't so smart after all. She felt stupid that she hadn't managed her money better and had allowed herself to get in such deep debt.

The solution to her problem was to make her debt go away. It seemed that bankruptcy did just that. She could eliminate her debts and start over with a fresh slate. And best of all, her parents would never know. Vanessa didn't even consider any other solutions to her problem because she was certain this answer was the ideal one. Alas, Vanessa hadn't yet taken a class in bankruptcy law. If she had, she would have been familiar with the fact that bankruptcy has numerous "cons" in addition to its obvious "pros."

The fact is that a Chapter 7 bankruptcy, which is the most common personal bankruptcy, will stay on your credit report for ten long years.

This entry will affect all future credit decisions and may cause you to be denied additional credit. Even if you are approved, the interest rate you will be charged will be much higher than average.

These consequences became all too apparent in Vanessa's post-bankruptcy years. Her bankruptcy first haunted her when she wanted to move from her dorm to off-campus housing. Every time a landlord pulled her credit report, her application was turned down. She had to be content with dorm living for a while longer. When Vanessa then tried to get a loan on a used car, she was denied at almost every car dealer on account of her bankruptcy. One dealer finally gave Vanessa approval on condition that she accept a 35 percent interest rate.

Ironically, one of Vanessa's main motivations for filing bankruptcy was keeping her parents in the dark. The secret that Vanessa had tried so hard to keep was begrudgingly disclosed when she was forced to tell her parents the truth. It wasn't that Vanessa felt a sudden need to be honest; she needed her parents to co-sign in order to get an affordable interest rate on her car loan.

Unless you have avoided your debt situation for such a lengthy period that all other options are no longer possible, there may be alternatives to bankruptcy that will get you out of your financial dilemma. Options like credit counseling, negotiating with creditors to work out a repayment plan, and asking friends and family for help may not be easy solutions, but then again neither is bankruptcy. Only after you have thoroughly exhausted all other alternatives should you consider a radical solution that you may live to regret.

54

Balance Your Checkbook

I've met people who have never balanced their checkbook. When the bank statement arrives, they just throw it in the garbage or put it in a file, never to be opened. Instead of keeping track of their accounts themselves, they leave it up to the bank. Many just wait until the bank tells them they are overdrawn, and then they stop spending until they receive their next paycheck.

This method of keeping track of your bank accounts is an expensive one. Most banks charge an overdraft fee or may even return a check marked NSF (not sufficient funds). In addition to the fee charged by the bank for the NSF check, you may also be assessed a fee from the creditor who is receiving your bounced check. This creditor's fee will be used to help defray the costs of reprocessing your check. If you maintain a consistent pattern of bouncing checks, even more dire consequences can occur, as Matt discovered.

Matt tried balancing his checkbook once. It turned out to be such a frustrating experience for him that he never attempted it again. Matt was a journalism major in college and math was a subject that was definitely not his forte. After graduation he started working as a reporter for a small-town newspaper in Iowa.

He rationalized that people were either good with numbers or they weren't. Since he was not of a mathematical mind-set, he avoided tasks that required math skills. Balancing his checkbook fell into the category of a task to be avoided at all costs. Besides, if the bank was already tracking all of his transactions, why was it necessary for him to double-check its work? He believed that if the bank made a mistake, someone would eventually catch it and make a corrective entry in his account.

Since human error is always a factor, I personally wouldn't want to always trust the bank. In fact, one year I caught an accidental double withdrawal that was posted on my account. I brought this to the bank's attention and it reversed one of the withdrawals. According to Matt's philosophy, my bank would have eventually caught the error, but I tend to be more skeptical.

Matt's total reliance on the bank extended to his spending patterns. Since he never really had an accurate idea of how much money was in his account, he just relied on the bank to stop him when the money wasn't there. For instance, he would just continue to withdraw money from ATMs until a message popped up on the screen that said he had "insufficient funds" for that transaction. Then he knew he had to wait until his next paycheck was deposited in order to have access to money again. Sometimes he had to wait only a few days, and on other occasions his wait was much longer.

If the wait was long enough, Matt turned to other sources of interim money. He either got a cash advance from his credit card or went to a payday loan company to get an advance on his future paycheck. Both of these options are costly, since cash advances are usually charged a higher interest rate than normal credit-card transactions and payday loan companies charge a high percentage fee for their services.

In addition to the debt and high fees Matt was incurring every time he ran out of money, he encountered a problem of a different nature when he started to bounce his checks. Since Matt paid for most of his bills with checks, he just wrote a check and hoped that he had enough money in his account to cover the amount. When this was not the case, the check bounced and he was charged $28 by his bank and usually a bounced-check fee from the company to whom the check was written. He routinely paid between $150 and $200 each month in NSF fees and other penalties.

Eventually Matt's bounced-check situation was so routine that his bank closed his account. When he tried to open an account at another bank, he was turned down. He discovered a report called "ChexSystems" that was similar to a credit report. The difference was that this report tracked your bank history and not your credit history. Matt's "ChexSystems" report was so bad that he found he couldn't get another bank account opened anywhere. He ended up being forced to cash his paychecks at a check-cashing office that took 5 percent of his paycheck to conduct this service.

Matt was very angry at his bank for getting him into this situation. He felt deceived because he had relied on the balance that was printed on his ATM receipts in order to know how much money was in his account. His checks should have been covered. What Matt didn't realize was that the balance printed on those receipts didn't always include outstanding checks that had not yet cleared or other withdrawals that had not been posted to his account.

Balancing your checkbook and continually keeping track of your transactions is the best way to give yourself more control over your finances. By recording your deposits, the checks you have written, and the cash withdrawals you have made, you can determine your running balance. You will then have a clear notion of what is in your account instead of it being a mystery. This knowledge will save you money by helping you avoid bounced check fees, cash-advance charges, and payday loan operations.

55

Don't Wait to Win the Lottery

It is important to remember that there are only two ways to make your financial situation better. You can either increase your income or decrease your expenses. By making a concerted effort to do both, you can even heighten your chances of improving your financial status. However, many people believe there is a third way.

This third way is not a tried-and-true path but more of a gambler's dream. It is waiting to win the lottery or receive an inheritance or marry a rich man. This way is desirable because it does not involve any account-ability or effort on the part of the person wanting to improve his or her financial situation. People with these hopes believe they don't need to make sacrifices by reducing their expenditures or working more hours to increase their income or going to night school to get a higher degree. The problem is that by waiting for someone else to save them, they might be waiting forever.

A nineteen-year-old single mother named Lara came in for credit coun-seling. She had charged her credit cards to the max and was having a hard time making all her payments and meeting expenses. Lara wasn't trying to collect child support, which would have helped her situation, because the father was a student and unemployed. He had graduated from high school and went on to college like she had planned to do prior to becom-ing pregnant. Because of her child, she had dropped out of high school and was living on welfare.

The counselor went over many options with Lara to increase her income. She could take advantage of free child-care programs, which would enable her to work. Another option was to continue her schooling at night and get her high school equivalency diploma. With a diploma, Lara could get a better job. Her relatives could watch her child during the evening after they came home from work. A case could be started with the district attorney's office to try and collect the child support owed her.

For one reason or another, Lara turned down every option. In exasperation, the counselor finally asked how she intended to make her financial situation better. She then mentioned an inheritance that she would collect after her grandmother died. This inheritance would solve all her financial worries. The counselor asked about her grandmother's health. Lara replied, "Great." The counselor then asked how old her grandmother was. She replied, "Sixty-three." The counselor then thought to herself, "Either Lara's going to be waiting a long time or she's planning something I don't want to know about!"

Lara was looking for someone else to save her—her grandmother. Considering her grandmother's health and age, the wait could be quite long. A better solution would have been for Lara to attempt to collect child support. This income could have significantly improved her situation. Many women don't try to collect support that is due to them. Consequently, their financial situation suffers as they try to support a child on their own. If they are young and haven't finished school, the financial demands are almost impossible to meet.

Who knows if Lara would have been successful in collecting child support, but at least she could have tried. Trying is actually the best way she could have increased her odds of a happy ending. Without trying, her only other option was to wait. I hope Lara has lots of patience.

Some people look to the lottery to save them. In reality, you have more chance of contracting a flesh-eating bacterial infection than winning the lottery. And the cost of continually buying lottery tickets adds up. If you buy them daily, how much do you spend in a week, a month, or a year? This is money spent on a dream, not anything concrete. While money spent on food and money spent on clothes always give you something in return, money spent on lottery tickets is gone without a promised return.

The lottery is only one form of obvious gambling. Other quick-fix hopes are betting at the horse tracks, playing slot machines, entering into a sports gambling pool, and playing blackjack. These are activities we automatically equate with gambling, but there are other forms that are much less obvious. These include picking a commission-only job, investing in a gold mine, and trying to marry into money. All these forms of gambling involve a great deal of risk.

The only guaranteed way to improve your financial situation is to become proactive and do the hard work that is necessary to either make more money or cut back on your spending. The hope of an inheritance, a windfall, or a knight in shining armor coming to the rescue is just that— a hope, not a guarantee.

56

Never Go to a Credit Repair Clinic

The desire to rid your credit report of negative information can lead to doing business with some unscrupulous firms. You may believe these firms are entirely legitimate. They advertise their services in reputable publications and have offices that are next to the dry cleaners or Subway sandwich franchise. However legitimate their appearance may be, their practices may be unlawful or at the very least unethical.

Credit repair clinics often promise to remove negative entries from your credit report for a fee, although the law clearly states that credit history that is negative can only be removed if the information is false. But people who have negative entries on their credit report may be willing to believe and try just about anything to get these negatives removed.

The knowledge of how powerful credit reports are usually comes after your credit report has already been blemished. It does no good to learn after the fact that late payments or nonpayments will harm your credit history. By that time, it is too late. Your payment pattern has already been documented.

Margaret only realized the power of a credit report when she tried to rent her first apartment. Every apartment manager she visited pulled her credit report and then promptly turned her down. It did no good to explain that she never realized paying late was so detrimental. She never thought it was a big deal to pay late. Wasn't the most important concern the fact that she *eventually* paid her bills? Evidently not, she discovered, since her applications were never approved.

Margaret was given the option to have her parents co-sign on her apartment lease, but she resisted that solution. She had just graduated from college and was adamant about making it on her own. Besides, she was trying to prove to her parents how responsible she was. Margaret was sure there must be another way out of her mess.

One day she was reading the classifieds and saw an ad that promised to erase the negative entries on her credit report—guaranteed! Although she was a little skeptical, Margaret hurried to the company's office. For a mere $500 they assured her that they would succeed in removing these irritants from her credit report. They told Margaret they would produce a copy of her credit report shortly with all the negative entries deleted. In fact, when she received the report, the entries were, as promised, miraculously gone! Her initial skepticism was replaced with the assurance that she had made the right decision to have the "experts" handle her situation.

With her negative credit situation seemingly resolved, Margaret was confused when a month later she got turned down for a credit card. Since the law allows you a free copy of your credit report when you are turned down for credit, Margaret requested a copy. Upon receiving it, she was stunned that the negative entries had reappeared!

Margaret couldn't understand how this could have happened and sped off to the credit repair clinic for an explanation. She was sure they could fix the error. However, upon arriving at the credit repair clinic, the office had been vacated. It was empty, with no forwarding address listed. Her attempts to reach them by phone only resulted in a "disconnected" message.

Not knowing what to do, Margaret called her friend Tricia, who worked for the state department of consumer affairs. Her friend first scolded her for not coming to her for advice in the first place. Then she offered Margaret the most probable explanation as to how the negative entries had disappeared and then reappeared on her credit report.

Tricia said that when an entry is disputed, the credit bureau checks into its validity. While this research is under way, the negative entry is in essence "cloaked." This term has been used in the TV series "Star Trek" to describe something that has become invisible. This means that the negative credit entries are invisible until the results of the investigation are released. If the negatives are actually true, they will be "uncloaked." Since Margaret's entries were accurate, they reappeared.

However, if they had been posted in error they would have been removed. But if this is the case, individuals can dispute the reported information with the credit bureau for no charge on their own and avoid the credit repair clinic's fee. The process is simple and does not require an "expert" to complete the steps. The credit reporting agency then researches the dispute, and if the information is indeed inaccurate the negative entry will be deleted automatically.

Keep in mind that if the negative information is true, there is no way to remove it from your credit report for up to seven years. Credit repair clinics may be successful in getting the entry removed temporarily while the dispute process is under way. However, by the time you discover the entry has reappeared and go to the credit repair clinic to demand a refund, you may find, like Margaret, that it has moved and left no forwarding address.

57

Never Go to a
Payday Loan Store

Payday loans are advertised as solutions to short-term money problems. For many people living on the edge, managing their finances is a constant battle between time and money. The victor is determined by whether at the end of the month there is "more month than money" or "more money than month." In other words, did your paycheck stretch long enough to last until your next paycheck or did you find yourself having to raid the cupboards in your kitchen for old dry pasta because you couldn't afford to go to the grocery store?

When I lived in Los Angeles I had an actor friend named George who was an expert at surviving when his money ran out. He had a dinner routine set up that rotated the restaurants he would show up at for the free food during their "happy hour." For the price of a beer he could eat at their unlimited buffet. Even though the food was of questionable nutritional value (nachos, fried cheese sticks, and buffalo wings), it still served to fill his stomach. George even resorted to entering movie theatres through the exit in order to skip paying the price of the ticket.

This method of surviving worked for a while until the movie theatre caught him sneaking into the exit and barred him from the theatre. George also developed high cholesterol from eating so many greasy, fatty foods. He was in search of another scheme when he saw a TV advertisement one night for something called "payday loans." The type of client they were appealing to fit George's profile exactly, and he wrote down their 800 number and promptly called it.

The next day he showed up at one of the company's offices and was given two choices. He could either write a postdated check for the amount of the loan plus a fee or assign his paycheck to the lender via electronic funds transfer and receive the amount of his paycheck minus their administrative fee. George chose to write a postdated check. In exchange, George got his money immediately.

George had never planned on becoming a regular customer. He thought that he would use the payday loan office as a backup whenever he ran short of cash. If George had honestly looked at his money management patterns, however, he would have noticed that his cash shortage was an ongoing problem instead of an occasional one. The bottom line was that George *always* ran out of money before his next paycheck arrived.

It never occurred to George to analyze his budget in order to figure out how much his monthly expenses exceeded his income. That understanding would have helped him to determine his options. If he was just a little bit short, he could have looked at eliminating or cutting down on a few of his expenses. If he was a lot short, he would have had to look at more drastic options like getting a roommate or maybe another part-time job.

Since George never bothered to do any budget calculations, he became a regular customer at the payday loan office. In fact, this source of money was so easy compared to the schemes he had concocted in the past that he started visiting the office more and more frequently. Before he knew it, he had been advanced several paychecks instead of just one.

George didn't worry, however, because his postdated checks would eventually be covered by his paychecks. This worked as long as George was employed. One day he went to work and received notice that all part-time employees were being let go. George had been employed only part-time so that he would have time to go to auditions and work as an "extra" the other days of the week. Unfortunately, when companies are experiencing hard times, it is the part-timers that are the first to go.

After George lost his job he was unable to reimburse the payday loan company for the checks that he had been advanced. Before he knew it, the payday loan company's collection department was calling him. George was able to work out payment arrangements over several months to pay back what he had been advanced. Unfortunately, this necessitated finding a full-time job. George was forced to put his acting career on hold for a while until he caught up.

Like George, if you need your next paycheck now and can't wait until payday, payday loans may be very tempting to you. This type of loan is offered at an estimated 5,000 to 6,000 stores nationally, with the average loan being $200. Other names for payday loans are check loans, hold-a-check, and payroll advance loans. Regardless of what the loans are called, they are all very expensive. Interest rates can be as high as 400 percent. You have, in fact, given yourself a pay cut just by obtaining one of these loans.

In addition to the high fees and interest rates attached, there is the issue of developing an addictive dependency on the payday loan. Once the pattern of borrowing starts, it may be difficult to break the cycle of advancing from one payday loan to another. You may become a regular customer. Breaking this dependency becomes as difficult as overcoming any other addiction. It would have been much easier to have just done a budget!

58

If You Have an overspending Addiction, Seek Help

When taken to the extreme, spending money can become an addiction like overeating, excessive exercise, or such excessive television viewing that you are commonly referred to as a "couch potato." The addiction is usually triggered to fill a void. The overeater may find comfort and pleasure in food. The excessive exerciser may have a poor body image and desperately want to change his shape. The chronic TV watcher might be lonely, and the programs may make her feel a part of the dramas on screen.

Overspending can be triggered by almost any emotion. Some people spend money to try to cure depression. Others shop when they are bored, lonely, or to give themselves a reward. Emotional purchasing is something we all experience from time to time. It only becomes a problem when it is constant and can't be stopped. For instance, if you can't afford it but continue to go on expensive shopping sprees, this could signal addictive behavior.

Everyone who knew Todd was envious. Even though he was just twenty-four years old, it seemed that everything he touched turned to gold. He had passed the bar exam on the first attempt and was working for a prestigious law firm. He drove a Mercedes and was engaged to a woman that he seemed to just adore, judging by the huge diamond on her finger. In addition, Todd had just bought a condo in a trendy part of Chicago. His expensive suits and wining and dining of his fiancée, Donna, signaled Todd's success to his friends and triggered their envy.

"How can one man have such good fortune?" was the question that everyone seemed to ponder. On top of it all, he seemed content with his life. Whereas some people are never happy with what they have, Todd seemed perpetually happy. It was a mystery to his friends, who struggled with the normal depression and frustrations that accompany everyday life.

Even to his family and friends, he always maintained his cheerful demeanor. When asked the common greeting, "How are you?" Todd always answered, "Wonderful." Donna developed a sense of assurance that everything was taken care of and under control. She had no idea what Todd's financial situation was, but she was quite confident that it was very healthy. Otherwise how could he afford her engagement ring, dinners out, and his new condo?

Only Todd knew the real truth. His gambling addiction had gotten out of control years ago. The losses, which were far more numerous than his wins, had always been covered up by his student loans. As long as he remained a student and could remain eligible for additional student loans, he had nothing to worry about. Unfortunately, Todd hadn't planned on what to do once he had graduated.

With his student loan source of money gone, Todd started gambling more often and placing higher and higher bets to try to cover his increasing losses. To compound his problem, six months after he graduated his student loans became due. His monthly payment was quite high because he had borrowed so much. He worked longer hours at his law firm as his worry intensified. Even though on the inside Todd was scared to death, no one could ever tell from the outside. They all thought it was normal for lawyers to work long hours. He hid his fears from everyone, including his fiancée.

When it became apparent to Todd that he was going to lose his condo, his car, and maybe his job through bankruptcy, the thought of his lies being uncovered was more than he could bear. To admit the truth to his family and friends was not a possibility; to Todd there was only one possible solution. So that night he broke off his engagement to Donna and moved to Miami.

This radical action was incomprehensible to his family and friends. How could a man with everything let it all go? His job, his fiancée, and his condo were all left behind so he could "find himself" in Florida. Todd chose to stay silent about the real reason for his flight. The pressure to be successful and not fail was overwhelming. If Todd had admitted his gambling addiction and disclosed his dire financial situation, it would have exposed the lie that he was living. It was easier to flee than be humiliated.

Once your actions toward money become an addiction, the logical and rational mind that is necessary to make wise money decisions will take a backseat to your emotions. Unfortunately, many decisions based solely on emotions are not the most prudent course of action. To leave everything he loved and valued behind and flee was probably not the most rational solution to Todd's dilemma. Todd could have gone to Gamblers Anonymous when he first realized he had a gambling addiction instead of continuing to get deeper in debt.

Seeking professional help to conquer an overspending addiction may be necessary to break the cycle. The underlying reason for the overspending needs to be unearthed before the addiction can be overcome. Racetracks and casinos can be avoided, but the urge to gamble will find a way unless it can be conquered.

59

Be Prepared for Worst-Case Scenarios

Insurance is not an option; it is a necessity. You may rationalize not needing insurance by telling yourself that you are healthy or a good driver. These facts may be true, but you never know when you could get sick or injured or hit by someone who is not as good a driver as you. Since we cannot predict life events, we should be prepared for the worst.

Many of us have insurance only if we are required to have coverage. For instance, most states have laws making car insurance mandatory. Or we might have insurance by default if the company we work for provides life insurance as an employee benefit. But when insurance is optional, most of us choose to take our chances.

This is exactly what Andy chose to do. Andy worked as a salesman for a mobile-unit rental company. His salary was weighted heavily in favor of his commissions. In fact, his base pay was so minuscule that it constituted a very small percentage of his paycheck. Since his sales figures determined his paycheck to such a great extent, he was highly motivated to perform.

Andy was an avid snow skier, and he escaped to the mountains outside of Denver almost every weekend. Andy loved to take risks, both professionally and personally. When it came to skiing, he pushed himself to take the most dangerous runs regardless of the weather conditions. It was during a heavy snowfall when his visibility was severely impaired that he lost control and hit a tree. The fall resulted in serious breaks to both of his legs. The resulting surgeries and follow-up therapy took almost six months before he was able to go back to work.

After Andy used up his sick days at work, he started to receive disability income from the state. Unfortunately, his base pay was used to calculate the amount of disability he received. Since his base pay was so low, so too were his disability checks. This harsh decrease in his take-home pay caused Andy to fall behind on his car payment and his mortgage.

Andy vaguely remembered being asked by his insurance agent after he purchased his condo if he wanted to acquire a disability policy in addition to his regular home insurance. Andy thought this was an unnecessary expense considering his young age and the fact that he rarely took a sick day. He decided to decline the coverage.

Andy now regretted that decision because his mortgage would have been paid if he had only taken out a policy. Instead, he found himself after the accident with a reduced income but no accompanying decrease in expenses. After withdrawing the maximum in cash advances from his credit cards, he ran out of income options. Being bedridden prevented him from doing moonlighting work.

Andy's one salvation was the fact that he continued to communicate with his creditors. He let them know about his short-term disability, and he was finally able to negotiate an accelerated repayment plan that started upon his return to work. He was able to make more than the required payment each month, and after a year he finally caught up.

Of course, Andy had to severely cut back on his expenditures for that year. No more fun—he had to direct almost all of his discretionary funds to his repayment efforts. This experience caused Andy to change his idea of insurance from a want to a need.

Two types of "optional" insurance that should be strongly considered are life and disability. Life insurance is particularly essential if you have dependents. If you died, how much would it cost to cover your family's expenses? You may not think life insurance is necessary if your employer already covers you, but consider the gap in coverage if you get laid off or change jobs. The most cost-effective type of policy for people in their twenties is term life insurance. This type of insurance pays a specified benefit when you die.

The second type of insurance to be considered is disability. The argument for disability insurance is best illustrated by the fact that "the odds of a thirty-five-year-old woman being unable to work for at least three months due to an injury or illness are five times higher than her odds of dying," according to the Social Security Administration. If your company already offers this benefit, you should read the fine print. Are the benefits only offered for a limited period, such as a year? If your disability is serious, a year may not provide enough coverage.

Carrying insurance is a way to have the peace of mind that if events occur and you need coverage, you will have it. Living without insurance is an incredibly risky way to go through life. If something tragic happens, you could be ruined financially by the huge expenses that you alone will be responsible for.

60

Resist Panic Decisions When the Market Is Down

When the stock market is not performing well, the tendency is to sell and cut your losses before it's too late. This short-term situation needs to be viewed in the long-term context. Over time, the stock market has outperformed every other savings instrument (bonds, savings accounts, CDs) over every ten-year time frame. From 1940 to 2001, the stock market was up forty-seven years out of sixty-two. In other words, about three out of every four years the market rises.

Dips in the market are to be expected. When this happens, resist making panic decisions that you will regret. It helps to focus on acting like an investor instead of a trader. A trader is someone who tries to make money on short-term buys and sales by taking advantage of fast changes in the market. An investor, on the other hand, views the short-term fluctuations in the market as irrelevant and follows a high-quality buy-and-hold policy. Heather got into trouble by acting like a trader instead of following a strategy of long-term investments.

Heather panicked when she received the quarterly statement from Charles Schwab that listed all her investments. Several of her mutual funds were down over 10 percent from the previous quarter. But she remembered her investment advisor's advice to view investing as a long-term commitment, so she did nothing. However, when she received her next quarterly statement and her funds continued their decline, now down another 10 percent, Heather decided to sell.

She had her investment advisor move her funds into safe government bonds. Immediately Heather felt a sense of relief. The anxiety she was experiencing watching her funds dip lower and lower was now replaced by the certainty of a 4 percent return on her money.

Heather didn't even look at the next quarterly statement she received, since her money was no longer at the mercy of fluctuations. She continued to ignore her subsequent quarterly statements also. It was only a year later that she happened to actually read her quarterly statement.

To Heather's horror, the mutual funds that had been down 10 percent each quarter had rebounded to a year-end increase of 15 percent over the previous year. This 15 percent increase was more than the 4 percent she was earning on her safe government savings bonds. If she had only taken her investment advisor's advice and done nothing, her investments would have shown a greater return for the year. Her panic reflex was responsible for an 11 percent decline in the value of her investment accounts.

Because we live in a society where success and accomplishments are often associated with an activity or action of some kind, when something isn't going exactly the way we want it to we feel the need to do something to fix it. Just keep in mind that sometimes the best thing to do is nothing.

The temptation among many investors is to get in quick, then get out quick, taking profits or cutting losses at a moment's notice. But by focusing only on the short term, many investors like Heather lose sight of the big picture. Performance over the long term instead of short-term gains or losses should be the motivation behind investing.

You need to learn to measure your success by how your portfolio is performing and not against market indexes like the Dow Jones or the S&P 500. For example, if your long-term plan requires your investments to earn around 12 percent a year, then it is irrelevant that the stock market index went up 25 percent. What matters is how your total portfolio is doing. Check periodically to make sure you are on track, and then ignore the craziness of the market.

Successful mutual fund and stock market investing requires one trait that seems to be lacking in many people—patience. An oft-quoted saying that bears repeating is, "It is time *in* the market, not timing the market, that will most likely produce the greatest profits in investing in the stock market."

Conclusion

My final piece of advice to you is "Take my advice." Learn the money rules!

I truly believe that money doesn't buy happiness. I used to work in Beverly Hills, California, and some of the unhappiest people I've ever met lived there. At first I couldn't understand how they could be so miserable. If I were in their shoes, certainly I would be ecstatically happy. But as I got to know many of my clients better, I discovered that money was not an automatic panacea for their problems.

They had the same problems that the rest of us had. They had work-related problems, family disputes, weight issues, traffic congestion, and all the other daily annoyances that we all face. But they also had additional problems brought about solely because of their wealth. They had squabbles over inheritances, suspicions of being overcharged for services, worries over their spouse-to-be's real intention in wanting to get married.

They say that when you are at the top, you spend most of your time trying not to fall. Ironically, although wealth can certainly lessen many worries (you don't have to worry about how to pay the bills), wealth brings with it concerns of its own. When you have wealth, you have to constantly worry about those who will try to take it away from you. You may become suspicious of people's intentions and become more cynical in your view of human nature. This is a sad by-product of wealth.

Even though I am convinced that money doesn't buy happiness, I strongly believe the reverse: that money problems bring unhappiness. My six years spent working at Consumer Credit Counseling Service confirmed this belief. Without exception, every client that came in for counseling with a serious financial problem was unhappy. How could they not be?

For money troubles bring a myriad of other troubles as well. Most marriages and relationships suffer while going through the strain of a financial crisis. When the parents are under money stress, their children will not easily escape feeling their parents' fear. Their safe and secure world has been disrupted, and this may cause them to feel a high level of anxiety.

Additionally, self-esteem issues surface during money troubles because so many of us link our wealth to our level of self-worth. Someone who is used to being the provider and now cannot support the family may experience anger and guilt. He or she may lash out at loved ones just because they are close by and therefore easy targets. If family members are angry at one another, the resulting strain on the family makes the financial crisis even harder to resolve: in order to solve money issues, it is imperative that everyone work together as a team.

Worrying over money can affect your quality of sleep as well. Many people find it difficult, if not impossible, to sleep when they have money troubles on their mind. The fatigue caused by sleepless nights may be compounded by an increase in blood pressure caused by the anxiety and stress. In severe cases, a heart attack may even occur.

Money worries cannot be escaped even when you're at work. Companies have found that workers who are worried about their finances tend to be less productive. This is understandable since it is hard to concentrate on the job if you are concerned with how you are going to pay the mortgage this month. It becomes even harder to concentrate if you are receiving calls from collection agencies while you're at work.

The best incentive to get your finances under control is that if you do, other areas of your life will improve also: your relationships, your job performance, and your health. As you slowly start to work your way out of financial problems, you will notice a gradual decrease in your stress level and corresponding increase in your happiness level.

Since eliminating money problems is the surest way to increase your happiness quotient, I advocate preventive education. It is easier to avoid a money problem in the first place than trying to work your way out of it after it has become a crisis. Most people don't understand money, so consequently they don't realize they are making mistakes until after they have made them.

Endeavor to become a master of your finances. This mastery will put you in control of your money, instead of your money being in control of you. You will learn how to become proactive in money matters—not just reactive. If you habitually receive collection calls, delinquency notices, and bounced-check notifications, you must constantly *react* to the situation, rather than taking a *proactive* approach.

The difference comes down to *when* you act. Proactive money managers act before there is a crisis, not after. The best way to become proactive is through familiarity with your financial situation. If you are truly aware of where you stand financially, you will be able to identify—and hopefully, prevent—a crisis before it erupts. Education is the key that will allow you to make the paradigm shift from having the future dictated to you, to having power over your financial future.

By learning and following the money rules in *Don't Spend Your Raise*, you will increase your odds of making fewer money mistakes and having more money successes. So I encourage you to follow the rules and start leading a more prosperous life.

Index